W ELLIOT BULMER graduated with an MA(Hons) in Arabic and Politics from the University of Edinburgh in 2000, and then joined the Royal Navy as a Logistics Officer. He saw service at sea in ships and submarines and spent six months leading a special operations (PSYOPS) team in Iraq. On leaving the Navy in 2006 he embarked on postgraduate studies at the University of Glasgow, focusing on constitutional design, while teaching undergraduate courses in comparative politics, history of political thought and nationalism. In addition to his research, teaching and writing, he has since 2008 been involved in the Constitutional Commission, of which he is currently Research Director and Vice-President. He is married and lives in Dunblane, where he enjoys communing with nature, reading, real ale and learning the banjo.

D0907890

Luath Press is an independently owned and managed book publishing company based in Scotland, and is not aligned to any political party or grouping.

# A Model Constitution for Scotland:
# Making Democracy Work
# in an Independent State

W ELLIOT BULMER

In association with the
Constitutional Commission

**Luath** Press Limited

EDINBURGH

www.luath.co.uk

First published 2011
Reprinted 2012

ISBN: 978-1-908373-1-37

The paper used in this book is recyclable. It is made
from low chlorine pulps produced in a low energy,
low emissions manner from renewable forests.

Printed and bound by
Bell & Bain Ltd., Glasgow

Typeset in 11 point Sabon
by 3btype.com

# Contents

# Acknowledgements

I WISH TO THANK the following people, without whom this book would not have been written: my supervisors at the University of Glasgow, Dr Thomas Lundberg and Prof. Andrew Lockyer, for their advice and guidance; Ian McCann for permission to access the SNP archives; the staff of the National Library of Scotland and of the University of Glasgow Library for their patient assistance; John Drummond of the Constitutional Commission for his positive vision and radical optimism; my parents and family for their encouragement and support; and, above all, my loving wife Eva Dominguez, who has helped in ways far too numerous to mention.

# The Constitutional Commission

THE CONSTITUTIONAL COMMISSION was founded in 2005 by John Drummond (former Convenor of the Independence Convention) and Kenyon Wright (former Convenor of the Scottish Constitutional Convention).

It is an independent, non-partisan charitable organisation dedicated to 'the advancement of education, citizenship and community development through a better understanding of constitutional structures, processes and improvements'.

## Research

At a time when independence, fiscal autonomy and other options are on the agenda in Scotland, the Constitutional Commission aims to understand the constitutional options available, to appreciate their nuances and their consequences, and to make recommendations which would improve the quality of our democratic life. We also seek to monitor institutional changes at the UK level from a Scottish perspective and to understand their effect on Scotland.

## Education

Scotland lacks constitutional literacy. The constitutional debate in Scotland is often partisan, short-sighted and ill-informed – hardly ideal conditions for bringing about a lasting democratic solution. The Constitutional Commission seeks to bring together academics from several disciplines, politicians from all parties, civic organisations and members of the public from all walks of life, in order to increase constitutional literacy, to digest research, and to deliberate and reflect on constitutional options.

## Promotion of Citizenship

The Constitutional Commission promotes democratic citizenship by highlighting the connection between a sound constitutional structure, effective democratic practices, and beneficial policy outcomes that serve the common good. We aim to promote understanding of the roles and responsibilities of citizens in a democratic Scotland.

www.constitutionalcommission.org

# Preface

THE IDEA FOR THIS book emerged shortly after the elections of May 2007, which brought a minority SNP Government to office in Holyrood. Although welcoming the Scottish Government's 'National Conversation' on Scotland's future, and keen for independence to be put to the people, members of Constitutional Commission were uneasy at the prospect of an independence referendum being held without prior thought being given to the Constitution of an independent Scotland. It was felt that achieving independence without constitutional reform could potentially reverse the democratic advances made since devolution, such as proportional representation, the balance of power between executive and legislature, and protection of human rights. In the absence of a proper written Constitution, an independent Scottish Parliament would be in a position of supreme, unlimited authority; a lamentable situation, that could easily lead to the concentration of excessive power in the Scottish Government, to the weakening of parliamentary and extra-parliamentary accountability mechanisms, and to the erosion of our civil liberties and human rights.

In response to these concerns, the Constitutional Commission decided that the most constructive way to bring these issues to the attention of decision-makers, opinion-formers and a wider Scottish public, was to elaborate detailed constitutional proposals in the form of a Model Constitution for Scotland. Producing a Model Constitution would facilitate a systematic exploration of all questions arising out of the design of a Constitution, providing comprehensive (if not final) answers, and offer a workable blueprint around which democrats could unite.

In offering support to this project, the Constitutional Commission is not necessarily endorsing independence, but is affirming its commitment to civic democracy and constitutionalism *in the event of* independence. The opinions expressed in this book are those of the author alone; they do not necessarily represent the views of the Constitutional Commission, nor those of its trustees, members or supporters.

*John Drummond*
Convenor, Constitutional Commission

# Introduction

THE CONSTITUTIONAL DEBATE in Scotland is focused almost exclusively on the 'status question' – the relationship between Scotland and the rest of the United Kingdom. The Scottish Government's 'National Conversation' has framed the debate solely in terms of a sliding scale of Scottish autonomy, ranging from the devolved status quo, through implementation of all or part of the Calman Commission proposals and some sort of 'Devolution Max', to independence. Little thought has been given to constitutional form of that future Scottish State might take in the event of achieving such independence.

If the painful political history of the 20th century teaches us anything, aside from the superiority of liberal-democracy over all forms of closed and tyrannical society, it is that independence and freedom are not synonymous. Too many States have achieved independent Statehood only to become entangled again with the yoke of bondage; their struggles for national independence have often been followed by a period of instability and violence, culminating in ideological tyranny, personal dictatorship, military rule, or a narrow squabbling oligarchy. If Scotland is truly to flourish, we need much more than just independence: we need a robust liberal-democratic polity, with an open, representative, accountable and constitutional form of government. We need to establish a civic and democratic order in which the common good can be discerned and realised.

While the chances of a stable democracy taking root in Scotland are also contingent upon many cultural and socio-economic factors which are outside of our immediate control, the quality and longevity of a democracy can be greatly influenced by its constitutional structure. It could even be argued that a good Constitution – not just in the form of words on a page, but as a living reality – is of first-order importance to the peace, freedom and well-being of the nation. Stable liberal-democracy under a good Constitution is what separates the success stories of 20th century independence (Finland, Norway, Ireland, Iceland, Malta) from the failures (Zimbabwe,

Pakistan, Burma).[a] Since this is the case, the absence of serious and informed debate on the future Constitution of an independent Scotland is a cause for concern.

This absence of debate on Scotland's constitutional future appears to be particularly puzzling when one considers the intellectual origins and the motivating ideas of the Scottish independence movement. The desire for Scottish independence has never been a narrowly nationalistic, ethnic, or separatist movement. Rather, it is a movement that, from the start, has advocated democratic renewal and constitutional government. What is called 'nationalism' or 'separatism' can perhaps better be understood as a campaign for democratic renewal and civic self-government.

The Scottish independence movement has been based on a tradition of the sovereignty of the people. This tradition sees sovereignty as inherently belonging to the 'whole community of the realm', in contrast to a key 'Hanoverian' concept of the British State – namely, the 'sovereignty of Parliament'. The origins of this tradition can be traced to the Declaration of Arbroath of 1320, in which the king was explicitly bound by and to the whole people. It also found expression in the Reformed tradition, with its concern for 'covenanted' relationships based on mutual responsibility and the limitation of all power by law. This is, of course, an historical fiction; there never was a medieval Scottish Republic, and there has never been a democratic Scottish Constitution that fully embodies the principle of popular sovereignty. Yet, if sovereignty of the people was never an historical reality, it has nevertheless become an incontrovertible moral claim that has been used to critique the authority of Westminster.

---

[a] The reputation of Iceland has been damaged by the financial crisis of 2008–2009. It is true that Iceland overstretched itself: the bubble burst, as all credit bubbles must do. However, the argument that these setbacks undermine the case for the independence of small nations cannot be accepted. Iceland, as long as she retains her democracy and independence, is well-placed to regain moderate prosperity in due course. If she is not, for the time being, part of the 'Arc of Prosperity', she remains a member of a more august and privileged club, the 'Arc of Democracy' – and democratic liberty is true wealth.

The SNP's commitment to liberal-democratic principles (and more specifically to a moderated, balanced form of democracy, characterized by power-sharing and genuine parliamentarism) was amply demonstrated by its development of a draft Constitution for an independent Scotland. When first published in 1977, the SNP's draft Constitution, known as the MacCormick Constitution, in honour of its principal author, Professor Neil MacCormick, marked a radical break from the then-prevailing British constitutional orthodoxy. It featured a Parliament elected by proportional representation, designed to encourage coalition government and to bring an end to artificially reinforced single-party majority rule. The Parliament was to be elected for fixed four-year terms, so that the Prime Minister would no longer be able to call snap elections to suit his own party's fortunes, nor cajole Parliament with the threat of arbitrary dissolution. In place of a hereditary or appointed second chamber, the Constitution proposed a novel 'minority-veto referendum' procedure, whereby two-fifths of the members of the Parliament would be able to suspend a bill, other than a money bill, for between 12 and 18 months. This delaying veto could, however, be overruled by a referendum. The monarchy was retained, but many prerogatives of the Crown were abolished or restricted. Instead of Westminster conventions regarding the appointment and removal of the Prime Minister, which could be problematic where no party has a clear majority, MacCormick's draft recommended a formal electoral process, whereby the Prime Minister would be chosen by a parliamentary vote, and would hold office unless removed by a vote of no-confidence. It also recommended that control of war-making and treaty-making powers be vested in the Parliament of Scotland, rather than in the Crown. The judiciary was also to be reformed. The MacCormick draft provided for the Court of Session to be given the status and authority of a proper Supreme Court, including the power to review the validity of legislation under the Constitution, and judicial appointments were to be made on the advice of an independent commission, whose members would be in part elected by Parliament. The Constitution contained a Bill of Rights closely modeled on the European

Convention, and the whole Constitution was presented in the form of a single, codified supreme law, which would be amendable only by a three-fifths majority vote of Parliament followed by a referendum.

Later versions of the SNP's draft Constitution made a number of minor changes, adding an article on local government, and increasing the prominence of socio-economic rights, but the underlying principles of the SNP's constitutional policy have remained unchanged for more than 30 years. These principles amount to a rejection of the Westminster model of politics in favour of a more 'Scandinavian' or 'Continental' alternative, which puts limits on the power of the Government and ensures greater accountability, representativeness, and protection for citizens' rights. In place of Westminster's disproportional single-party majorities, the SNP has always insisted that Scotland should have an inclusive Parliament elected by proportional representation. Instead of replicating in Scotland Westminster's autocratic Prime Minister and ineffective Parliament, the SNP has long demanded a more equitable balance of power between Government and Parliament in an independent Scotland – curtailing the Prime Minister's prerogatives and increasing the legislative and scrutinising role of Parliament. Likewise, in place of parliamentary sovereignty, the SNP has always demanded an entrenched Constitution to protect the rights of citizens and to clarify the ground-rules of political life.

In 2002, an SNP policy paper accompanying the most recent version of MacCormick's draft Constitution stated the party's commitment to these reformist principles in unequivocal terms:

> In line with practically every other country in the world, an independent Scotland will have a written constitution. A written constitution is necessary to protect the rights of every Scottish citizen and to place restrictions on what politicians can and can't do. A written constitution for a free Scotland provides us with an opportunity to enshrine fundamental human rights in Scotland's basic law and ensure a government truly accountable to the people of Scotland.[1]

Neil MacCormick described these ideas as the 'common stock of democratic thought in Scotland today'[2] – the foundation on which the Scottish State must be built.

However, the Scottish Government's White Paper, 'Your Scotland, Your Voice' (2009), while putting forward a strongly convincing case for independence, made only indirect, lukewarm commitments to democratic constitutionalism. According to the White Paper, Scotland could gain independence with only a few incidental changes to our current political institutions. All that would be required is the repeal or amendment, by the Westminster Parliament, of the offending parts of the Scotland Act and the Act of Union: abolishing the concept of 'reserved matters', prohibiting appeals to the British courts, and, in short, giving the Scottish Parliament sovereignty over all aspects of policy (subject, as applicable, to EU law and to the European Convention on Human Rights). There would, of course, be many incidental matters to be settled as part of the transfer of sovereignty, from the apportionment of national debts, through the status and pensions of UK civil servants in Scotland, to the division of military assets, but none of these would affect Scotland's form of government.

If that were the end of the matter, it would be wholly unacceptable. Independence under such conditions would merely replace the sovereignty of Westminster with that of Holyrood. No sincere democrat, who believes in the sovereignty of the people, recognises the importance of democratic accountability, and acknowledges the need to protect human rights from the expediency of those in power, could, in good conscience, accept such an outcome. A plenary transfer of power to a sovereign Scottish Parliament would only perpetuate the worst failings of the Westminster system, and do little or nothing to establish a just democratic order based on concern for the common good. This would not only squander a rare and valuable opportunity for reform, but would also betray the democratic values which, as noted above, have for decades been central to Scotland's grievance against the UK.

Fortunately, however, that is not the end of the matter. The SNP has not changed its policy; it maintains its long-standing commitment to liberal-democratic constitutionalism and remains pledged to the adoption of a written Constitution based on the draft prepared by Neil MacCormick. Full assurances to this effect have been given by Scottish Ministers[3]. The White Paper, although framed in the cautious and less emphatic terms of a Government, rather than a party, document, even hints in this direction:

> An independent Scotland could consider further progress, for example... ...formulating and agreeing a fully codified and written constitution. These issues would be decided within Scotland, either by the Scottish Parliament, or, as at the moment for major constitutional change, through a referendum.[4]

So a Constitution for Scotland is still very much on the agenda, but the detailed elaboration of the new Constitution appears to have been postponed until after independence. In some ways, this postponement is quite understandable. It reflects, in part, a desire to focus on what is seen as the central question – that of independence – without the distraction of other, post-independence, constitutional issues. In other ways, however, it could indicate a worrying lack of constitutional concern and awareness amongst senior civil servants, parliamentarians and other policy-makers – an inability to appreciate the fundamental difference between a 'sovereign Scottish Parliament' and a 'sovereign Scottish people', a misplaced belief that the mechanics of constitutional design are irrelevant to the health of a democratic society, or a cavalier expectation that the 'fiddly details' of constitution-making can be left to the discretion of constitutional lawyers.

Postponing the design of a Constitution until after independence is a risky and unsatisfactory course of action. A newly-independent Scottish State will suddenly have to deal with a range of immediate and practical problems, ranging from the establishment of embassies and the organisation of the armed forces to the issuing of postage stamps. Good constitutional design, so essential to the health of our polity, is likely to be forgotten in the rush.

Moreover, after three centuries of rule from Westminster, Scotland is ill-prepared for the delicate task of designing a new Constitution. We are a constitutionally illiterate country. We lack any direct experience of life under a Constitution, so we struggle to imagine how a constitutional government might operate in this country. We do not, generally speaking, even possess a basic constitutional lexicon – the framework of words and concepts with which to engage in the detailed discussion of constitutional questions. Most of us (and not just ordinary members of the public, but also many lawyers, politicians, civil servants, journalists and academics) have never *seen* or *read* a Constitution. Perhaps this is part of the reason why so few can see over the horizon of independence to consider what sort of Constitution Scotland will need thereafter. While not lacking in common sense or goodwill, we simply lack the knowledge to make good judgements on matters of constitutional design. That lack of knowledge breeds uncertainty, fear and avoidance of the issue. Even many of those who, in principle, support the idea of a Constitution are unsure about what a Constitution should contain, or else see it as a question of administrative detail, to be worked out by lawyers and civil servants, rather than as the fundamental political self-expression of a free, civic community.

This failure to 'grasp the thistle' of constitutional design, ahead of any referendum on independence, would enable the opponents of independence to claim (with some justification) that independence would be hazardous, as it would hand over indeterminate power to the Scottish Government without any thought of the consequences. It is too easy for the unionists to say that the implications of independence have not been properly thought through – that the people of Scotland are better off as they are, and that the campaign for independence is motivated only by the ego of 'narrow-minded separatists', rather than by a genuine hope for a better political system.

Furthermore, postponement increases the danger of ending up with a poor quality Constitution. The Constitution of a State must be well-designed from the outset. If this is not done, the parties and other vested interests will inevitably choke necessary reform; old abuses will continue, new ones will arise. Such an ill-set Constitution will give pain and discomfort for years to come. This being the case, the Government's failure to publish a Constitution for Scotland before the independence vote should be a matter of some concern to all supporters of Scotland's freedom.

The time to think about the future Constitution of an independent

Scotland, and to build a broad political and public consensus around an agreed constitutional text, is *now*, before a referendum on independence is held. This ought to be a matter of priority for the Scottish Government, for the SNP, and for all who support independence. It ought also to be given due consideration by those who would rather *not* see an independent Scotland, but who, if it happens, want to make it work. An effort should therefore be made to reach out to forward-looking and moderate unionists, who might not necessarily desire independence, but are willing to accept it and to work with it if it happens.

The purpose of this book, then, is not to offer arguments for Scottish independence, but to examine the best form of Constitution for Scotland *in the event* of independence. In dealing with this question, the book adopts an uncompromisingly and unapologetically normative tone; it is concerned not only with the mechanics of a technically sound constitutional design (although that is crucial), but also with the moral and political principles that make a Constitution 'good' rather than 'bad'. Liberal-democracy is presented not just as a procedural framework of decision-making, but also as a humane ethos and civic culture that governs how public decisions ought to be made. The aim is to ensure that an independent Scotland is also a free, flourishing and fair Scotland – a Scotland that enjoys stable civic-democratic politics, that empowers the people while protecting the rights of each person, and that promotes justice, peace, moderate prosperity and the common good.

These democratic ethical principles are rooted in the Scottish civic tradition, and are likely to be welcomed by a broad spectrum of Scottish opinion, transcending the divisions of class, geography, region and party politics. But principles only go so far. We may talk about the importance of representativeness, the rule of law, or accountability, but such talk is empty unless we can create the constitutional institutions through which these principles can be translated into political, social and legal practice. For example, if we agree on the desirability of democratic accountability, we must turn our attention to such dull details has how parliamentary committees are to be formed, how the auditors to inspect public finances are to be appointed, and what powers the ombudsman and public enquires ought to have. Likewise, if we agree on the need for participatory politics and a stronger civic spirit, we must study those constitutional devices that enable and encourage greater participation, such as referendums and the devolution of power to our cities.

The Model Constitution presented in this book is intended to give the principles of civic-democracy some precise institutional shape. It is a diligent attempt to apply the 'best practices' of constitutionalism and of parliamentary democracy to the current circumstances of Scotland and to practical realities of Scottish statehood. It is a 'Model' Constitution in the sense of being an example: it shows the people of Scotland what a good Constitution for Scotland *might* look like. It is also a model in the sense of being comprehensive 'working model', complete in every detail, which if desired could be adopted as it stands without requiring any further legal draftsmanship. It shows, therefore, that a good Constitution is not only possible, but also, given a basic understanding of the subject, quite easy to achieve. The term 'Model' does not, however, imply any pretence to perfection. The author does not claim the final word on this subject, but merely hopes to excite public interest and spark a more constructive constitutional debate, from which further improvements may well result.

Those who design a Constitution for a new State must make choices on several levels. First come the macro-choices, the 'choices of principle' which determine the purposes of the Constitution. Only then can we consider which meso-choices ('choices of structure') and micro-choices ('choices of detail') are best suited to achieve those purposes in a given time and place.[5] The first part of this book therefore discusses the principles and basic structures of a Constitution for Scotland. The second part deals with the detailed provisions of the Constitution, including the composition, organisation and terms of office of Parliament, the electoral system, the formation and removal of the Government, the judiciary, the ombudsman, local government, the role and functions of the Head of State, the rights of the people, and the means of holding the Government to account. Throughout, a constant theme of the book is that the best case for independence rests not on appeals to nationalism, but on a commitment to a vision of Scotland based on the universal ethical principles of democracy.

## PART ONE

# Introductory Notes

# A Civic Approach to Democracy

BEFORE COMMENCING THE design of a Model Constitution for Scotland, we must address the essential question: 'What sort of country should an independent Scotland be?' This question leads us to consider the basic assumptions, aims, values and principles of the political, legal and socio-economic *regime*. Is Scotland to be an authoritarian one-party State? A feudal monarchy? A military dictatorship? A Soviet Republic? A Calvinist theocracy? An oligarchy of international bankers and corporate interests? Or is it to be a constitutional and civic liberal-democracy?

It is quite tempting to reject all but the last of these regime-types out of hand, and thus to assume that the nature and the advantages of liberal-democracy are self-evident. After all, we claim to live in a liberal-democracy (albeit an imperfect one), and support for liberal-democracy unites almost all parties and interests in Scotland. Scottish politics has long been inspired by liberal-democratic motives, and public demand for constitutional change in Scotland, from the Chartist movement to the Claim of Right of 1989 and the setting up of the Scottish Parliament, has consistently been in the direction of more liberal-democracy, not less.

Yet the moral case for liberal-democracy still needs to be made. Popular acceptance is of course necessary, but it alone cannot make an unjust regime just. When distinguishing between good forms of government and bad or corrupt forms, it is necessary to consider the nature, purpose and effect of the regime, and not merely its popular acceptance. We need to understand why liberal-democracy is a *good thing*, and why an elected dictatorship, even if endorsed by a large majority, cannot be regarded as a legitimate or just form of government.

To do this, it is first necessary to define our terms. Liberal-democracy is a complex and contested concept that may be interpreted in various ways. Nevertheless, at the most basic level, it could be defined as: a system of collective self-government which features representative participation in, and ultimate popular control over, the decision-making authorities of State and society, combined with the protection of civil, legal and personal rights under the rule of law. The first part of this definition, focussing on public participation, popular control and accountability, is the 'democratic' aspect of liberal-democracy. The second part, concerning basic rights and the rule of law, is the 'liberal' aspect. Although there is inevitable tension between these two principles, both must be present for liberal-democracy to exist.

Robert Dahl specifies eight criteria of liberal-democracy which enjoy widespread acceptance:[6] (i) the right to vote; (ii) the right to be elected; (iii) the right of political leaders to compete for support and votes; (iv) free and fair elections; (v) freedom of association; (vi) freedom of expression; (vii) alternative sources of information; and (viii) institutions for making public policies which depend on votes and other expressions of preference.[7] To this one might add some other necessary features which Dahl may have taken for granted, such as: (ix) an independent judiciary which upholds the rule of law and (x) an impartial civil service.[8] To make democracy truly effective, we might also need to include matters such as local autonomy, the existence of widespread education, and restrictions on the extent of economic inequality. Yet, at an elementary level, these criteria (which, as can be seen, include both the democratic and the liberal elements) denote the universally recognisable features of modern liberal-democracy.

Many of the arguments in favour of liberal-democracy are derived from what is known as the 'contractarian' tradition. Although this tradition finds its fullest expression in the writings of the English Whig philosopher John Locke, its roots can be found in earlier Scottish writings. The Declaration of Arbroath, with its concept of a mutual obligation between the king and people, is steeped in medieval contractualism, while Scottish thinkers like George Buchanan and Samuel Rutherford had already given contractarian ideas a distinctly Presbyterian hue several decades before Locke wrote. In essence, the contractarian tradition relies on the idea of an original (real or notional) contract between the people and the State. This is supposedly drawn up by autonomous and rational individuals, each enjoying natural rights and equality under natural law. Coming together through the contract, the people empower the State to protect their natural rights, and in particular their property rights, while simultaneously prohibiting despotic government. If the State breaches this notional contract (for example, by ruling in an arbitrary manner, or by violating the rights which it is supposed to uphold) then the people are absolved of all obedience and can legitimately revolt in defence of liberty.

Contractarian ideas have historically provided a potent liberal antidote to the excesses and abuses of power. The Dutch Act of Abjuration of 1581, the Scottish Claims of Right of 1689 and 1989, and the American Declaration of Independence of 1776 – four documents which have an undeniable place in the history of liberal-democracy – all owe much to contractarian thought. However, the case of liberal-democracy does not depend on the acceptance of contractarian ideas: it can also be made on other theoretical, philosophical and theological grounds, which reject the individualist assumptions of Lockean liberalism.

Indeed, in recent years, over-reliance on contractarian principles has been increasingly criticised by civic-republican and Christian Democratic scholars, as well as by those on the socialist and Green left. Their concern is that the contractarian focus on rugged individualism can undermine the communal, fraternal, civic and ethical aspects of democracy. By reducing liberal-democracy to a means of protecting private rights, at the expense of public goods and of the commonweal, contractarian discourse can result in a shallow, 'procedural' liberty, which is devoid of substance, humanity and redeeming purpose.[9]

It is not possible or necessary to examine all these alternative, non-contractarian, arguments for liberal-democracy here. Instead, two simple and pragmatic arguments, drawing freely on a synthesis of both the civic republican and the Christian Democratic traditions, will suffice to show why liberal-democracy is the best form of government.

These might be termed the 'argument from results' and the 'argument from character'.

The argument from results asserts that liberal-democracies perform 'better' than other forms of State. Performance, in this case, must be assessed not just in narrow economic terms, but more broadly, in terms of their tendency to serve the common good rather than the personal good of the rulers. By requiring, at an absolute minimum, that those who govern be in some way chosen by and accountable to the people, and that basic civil liberties and human rights are upheld, the government of liberal-democracy can be relied upon to serve the public good to a greater extent than in non-democratic regimes. National resources are more likely to be channelled into projects that actually benefit the public, rather than those which flatter the ego of the leader. Mistakes are more likely to come to light, to be debated, and corrected. Various opinions and perspectives can be brought to bear on decision-making, and the decision, if not ideal, will at least be acceptable to large sections of the population. These views are reflected in the empirical evidence: high quality democracies, characterised by a high degree of power-sharing, spend more on health, education and welfare transfer payments, and less on instruments of state repression (police and armed forces) than less democratic regimes.[10] As Maurizio Viroli puts it:

> If public deliberations concerning the entire city are entrusted to councils representing the entire citizenry, it is more likely that sovereign decisions will affirm the common good, rather than the personal interests of rulers.[11]

Leaving aside the fact that enlightened despots tend to be succeeded by vicious and incompetent tyrants, and that even aristocracies of virtue tend to degenerate after a few generations into corrupt, self-serving oligarchies, one could argue democracy is not necessarily the best way to achieve the public good – that a gifted one or talented few might be able to identify the public good with greater clarity of vision, and to pursue that good with greater determination and singularity of purpose, than is possible in the noisy evolutions of a liberal-democracy. It is true, of course, that even the most thoroughly democratic of liberal-democracies will require the guidance of experts and the wisdom of its most excellent citizens if it is to flourish. Every good constitution is, to that extent at least, a 'mixed' constitution, harnessing the best and brightest (the true aristocracy of excellence) in the service of democracy.

Yet it is here that the argument from character comes into its own, and sets the bold, noisy contestation of liberal-democracy above the silent, invisible rule of the boffin and the bureaucrat. John Stuart Mill argues that liberal-democracy does not just deliver *better policies*, but also produces *better people*.[12] By asking people to participate in the deliberative realisation of their own public good, it produces active, responsible people. It makes people into the authors and producers, not merely consumers, of the common good. It asks us to consider the needs of our community, to judge the actions or inactions of our authorities, and to vote, protest, strike, campaign and participate, as necessary.

Democracy, at its best, lifts us from passivity into action, from selfishness into civic concern, from corruption into virtue. It does this by not merely reflecting our current wills or interests, but by forcing us to deliberate over these, to share them with others on grounds of reasoned public debate, and to seek common ground; it helps us to be more fully *human*, more authentically *humane*, and more charitably *humanitarian*.

A good liberal-democratic Constitution must, then, be designed with these two complementary ends in view: to promote well-being (Greek: *eudaemonia),* and to cultivate excellence (Greek: *arete*). Strictly speaking, such a democracy might be termed a 'civic-liberal-democracy', since it does not merely seek to protect pre-existing private rights, but rather to promote public goods. It seeks not the hollow freedom of the market-place, reduced to a choice between similar political products like that between two rival brands of cola. Neither does it offer the purely negative freedom to be left alone and shift for ourselves in an indifferent, uncaring world, as some extreme libertarians would have us believe. Rather, it strives for the freedom of the mature, morally responsible person, who is aware of their interdependence with their neighbours, their community, their country, and the world, and who seeks freedom to do what is right in concert with others. Only in such a civic-minded democracy can people 'own' their country, and so love it, and care for it, as a farmer owns his own fields or a shopkeeper his own shop. Only the citizens of a civic-democracy can exercise *caritas reipublicae* (loving care towards their Constitution, laws, liberties, and democratic institutions) and *caritas civium* (loving care towards fellow citizens).[13]

This mature and civic understanding of freedom has other lofty associations which, though largely forgotten, ought to be recalled. Firstly, freedom is linked to frankness. Free citizens are not subject to the grace and favour, or the arbitrary caprice, of anyone superior to them in power or rank. Citizens can speak plainly and boldly, treating all as their equals.

Secondly, free citizens are 'enfranchised', a medieval term denoting the *status* of a freeman. Enfranchised citizens do not have mere *power*, as despots do, nor are they merely *free from constraint*, as are outlaws and pirates. Instead, they have recognised, enforceable rights and privileges, based on their status as equal members of a self-governing community.

Thirdly, freedom is related to friendship. Only amongst free people, who can dare to be frank with one another, can the trust and friendship which makes civic life possible exist: those who do not enjoy such freedom, who fear that the 'intelligence service' is listening to their conversation, or that their 'friend' might turn out to be an agent of the secret police, cannot have the trust necessary to build a civic life. To break down such bonds of trust and friendship is the ultimate form of 'divide and conquer'.

Finally, freedom is related to peace. Freedom means not only the negation of slavery, but also all the destruction of all the apparatus of force and fraud that is necessary to sustain slavery: violence, oppression, torture, disappearances, deceit, corruption, injustices and fear. There is no peace in chains. Without freedom, a society lives in a state of war against itself, in which people may be devoured and destroyed for *raison d'etat*, to settle scores, to silence dissent, or to enrich the lucky few. A free State puts an end to that, and declares civil peace with its own citizens.

For these reasons, democracy cannot afford to remain neutral on all moral questions. Toleration and individual judgment are central liberal-democratic principles, but if a liberal-democratic State is to survive and thrive, it must ultimately acknowledge, at a basic constitutional level, what freedom is *for*. Freedom is valuable, firstly, because it enables us to pursue the common good (argument from results) and, secondly, because it helps us to be excellent human beings (argument from character). We do not seek freedom so that we can please ourselves, but so that, as fellow-citizens of a free and just community, we may love and serve one another, and through such love and service, can grow into ourselves and become as good as we can humanly be. Freedom, thus understood, is a serious ethical vocation, which requires us to cultivate good character and civic virtues. It cannot and must not be mistaken for amoral license, its cheap counterfeit.

In achieving these goals, a Constitution must work with the raw materials at hand – human nature, with all its human flaws, follies, and foibles. As many great philosophers of human freedom have consistently reminded us,[14] a good Constitution must strive to bring out our best, but still be prepared for our worst; it must guard against the corruption of the few and the apathy of the many; it must reward honourable public service, but punish the ambition to dominate; it must produce democratic leaders who can lead without tyranny or arrogance, and democratic citizens who can be loyal without being servile.

Bringing these aspirations back down to the realities of designing a Model Constitution for Scotland, three initial observations can be made. Firstly, the Constitution should not merely be designed to establish legal-procedural freedom, but also to create deliberative political 'spaces' where the *practice* of freedom as self-government can become a reality, and in which personal excellence can flourish: local democracy, direct democracy, and consultation with social interests, are potential manifestations of this ideal.

Secondly, constitutional rights and duties should also be structured around this teleological view of freedom. For example, freedom of speech is of vital importance. It is protected, albeit to varying degrees, in all liberal-democracies. However, the reason for freedom of speech is not, primarily, so that we can twitter our lives away – although that might be a pleasantly diverting consequence. Its chief importance is to equip us to maintain our freedom, to pursue the public good, and to uphold justice. Freedom of speech enables us to expose, criticise, and correct, the misguided actions of the powerful. It enables us to contest for the truth, and thereby to prevent a few from manipulating the public through error and imposition. It also helps us to become excellent, by expanding our knowledge and understanding. Hence not all restrictions on freedom of speech should be treated equally: a law restricting the right of advertisers to make misleading claims for their products, or to prevent the monopolisation of media ownership, does not infringe freedom in this civic democratic sense; indeed, it might actually help freedom to thrive.

Thirdly, this understanding of freedom means that the Constitution should not be viewed merely as a legal text – of interest to a handful of constitutional lawyers and bureaucrats, but irrelevant to most of the citizens in their daily lives. Rather, it should be regarded as a declaratory text, the foundational charter of the nation's free and civic way of life, which expresses in lasting and practical form the highest aspirations of the people. A good Constitution should unite the people when they are divided, recall them to their better selves when they are momentarily distracted by fear or anger, and set the standard for their shared political life when they are tempted by corruption. A good Constitution is thus not merely a rule in the sense of a blind set of 'rules of procedure'; it also contains something of the essence of a monastic 'rule' – an ethical basis that sets forth the shared goals and common standards of the community.

# What is a Constitution?

THIS DISCUSSION LEADS us to define more precisely what we mean by the term 'Constitution'. For some, the word can be applied to the cobweb of laws, institutions, principles, practices, traditions and conventions, which together constitute, or rather describe, the normal operating practices of government. This typically British definition of 'constitution' is very unsatisfactory. It is infinitely elastic: no breach of the traditional and unwritten 'constitution' can be punished, prevented, or even clearly identified. Such a 'constitution' merely describes a practical reality that is shaped, and can be moulded, by the will of the incumbent authorities; each breach becomes a new norm. If we accept this British definition of a 'constitutions', we must accept that the Emperor's 'New Clothes', in Andersen's fable, were fine examples of old-fashioned Westminster-cut tailoring: just as the Emperor's clothes were seamless, lightweight and totally breathable, so the United Kingdom has a constitution which is unwritten and unenforceable. It leaves us unprotected against the Government of the day.

Across the rest of the liberal-democratic West, including all of Europe and most former British colonies, the word Constitution implies something more specific. As Strøm *et al* point out:

> [Constitutions are not] mere behavioural regularities that reflect habit, tradition, or self-interest. Such patterns may persist as long as the actors in question find them profitable or convenient, but have no force or compulsion if that is no longer the case. [...] Therefore, for a rule to qualify as a mechanism of delegation or accountability, it must be enforceable. Voters, politicians, or civil servants must expect such rules to be backed up by direct or indirect sanctions from their principals, or from courts or other third parties that can enforce them.[15]

A Constitution, in the proper sense of the word, is the supreme and fundamental law, by which the sovereign constituent power (ultimately, the people, or, in a federation, the constituent States) establishes the constituted powers (the Parliament, Government and other institutions). A Constitution establishes, rather than merely describes, the rights and duties of the people, the powers and functions of the various institutions of government, and the relationships between them. A Constitution, by this definition, will usually also include a mechanism for its own amendment which is more complex and rigid than the mechanism for making ordinary laws, and will necessarily establish a body – such as a Supreme Court or Constitutional Tribunal – which has the authority to strike down any laws or other enactments which are deemed to be contrary to the Constitution.

The latter definition of Constitution, which will be used as our starting point, was popularised throughout the English-speaking world by Tom Paine in his 1791 publication, *The Rights of Man*. Thomas Paine defined a Constitution as:

> ... the body of elements to which you can refer, and quote article by article; and which contains the principles on which the government shall be established, the manner in which it shall be organised, the powers it shall have, the mode of elections, the duration of Parliaments... ...and, in fine, everything that relates to the complete organisation of a civil government'.[16]

As Paine noted, an unwritten Constitution, which cannot be produced on paper and quoted chapter and verse, is not really a Constitution at all. Likewise, a Constitution that is capable of being easily changed or overridden by the ordinary process of legislation is not worthy of the name. Thus, by Paine's definition, all talk of a 'British Constitution' is nonsense, for, as Paine continues, 'no such thing exists, or ever did exist'.[17]

Britain, uniquely amongst the nations of Europe, stumbled into mass democracy without pausing to adopt a fundamental, written Constitution. Instead, we got a 'sovereign Parliament', able through its almighty legislative power to do almost anything possible, except to place limits upon its own godlike power. Like Brahma, Vishnu and

Shiva, the King, Lords and Commons could create, sustain and destroy laws, rights and privileges at will. Owing to universal suffrage, this was called 'democratic'. In fact, the people had (and have to this day) no guarantee of their democratic rights, since rather than delegating powers to a limited Parliament under the fixed terms and conditions of a Constitution, as in other countries, the people are required at each general election to entirely abdicate their sovereignty to Parliament, with no guarantee that their interests will be pursued or their liberties upheld. Jean Jacques Rousseau, from the City Republic of Geneva saw through this sham in 1762. As he put it:

> the people... ...regards itself as free; but it is grossly mistaken; it is free only during the election of members of parliament. As soon as they are elected, slavery overtakes it, and it is nothing. The use it makes of the short moments of liberty it enjoys shows indeed that it deserves to lose them.[18]

A written Constitution is a necessary consequence of the principle of popular sovereignty, since it is only by establishing a superior constitutional law, enacted by the people and enforced by the courts, that Parliament and the Government can be prevented from usurping sovereignty and violating the people's rights. A written Constitution for Scotland is not, therefore, a radical idea; it is an ordinary, common sense idea, towards which both reason and many European examples guide us. The SNP, understanding this, has demanded a written Constitution for many decades (a demand that has been shared, with varying intensity, with other parties, including the LibDems and the Scottish Green Party).

Of course, we must be realistic about what we can expect a good Constitution to achieve. Even an 'ideal' Constitution, if such a thing could ever exist, would be no more than an indirect benefit. A Constitution cannot *directly* build a mile of road or educate a child. Yet the indirect benefits of a good Constitution can be seen throughout all spheres of a nation's economic, civil, social and cultural life. By ensuring that the public authorities are properly moderated, directed, and held accountable, a good Constitution enables them to faithfully serve the public, and causes them to do all that must be done for the common-weal, without becoming oppressive or lethargic. A good Constitution preserves peace by diffusing and settling conflicts, promotes harmony by enabling structured agreement to be achieved, and upholds justice by protecting the equal right and dignity of all. Moreover, a good Constitution (one which enables and requires us to act responsibly as citizens, and not only as passive consumers) develops our virtue, intelligence and excellence of character. It helps us, in other words, to achieve the 'good life': that is, to flourish as members of a free and flourishing community, and thus to realise our potential as *humane* beings. It is not a quick-fix panacea, but the long-term socio-economic, moral, cultural and political advantages of a good Constitution are immeasurable and undeniable.

# Consensus vs Majoritarian Democracy

HAVING AFFIRMED OUR commitment to a civic form of liberal-democracy as the only viable and acceptable form of government for Scotland, and having clarified our desire for a written and supreme Constitution, we can now begin to examine the institutional structures that such a Constitution ought to establish. Here the essential choice is between two models of democracy, the 'majoritarian' model and the 'consensus' model – a distinction developed by the Dutch political scientist Arend Lijphart.

Majoritarian democracies, patterned on the Westminster system, are characterised by the concentration and centralisation of power in the hands of a Prime Minister, who directs his Cabinet, is dominant over Parliament and is, between elections, unlimited by counterbalancing institutions. Consensus democracies, on the other hand, are characterised by the sharing, balancing and limitation of power. As the name implies, consensus democracies seek to govern by the sharing of power, with Parliaments elected by proportional representation, broad-based coalition Governments, and consultative, agreement-seeking approaches to policy-making. They also seek to limit the scope of the central State by means of decentralised local government, a rigid Constitution, bill of rights, and strong judicial review.

The traditional received wisdom, in Britain at least, proclaimed the superiority of the majoritarian model. It was deemed to produce a strong Government, clear choices, and an occasional alternation in office between two large, moderate parties. Even today, the defenders of the traditional British system will often concede that consensus democracies, with their proportional electoral systems and multi-party governments, are theoretically fairer and more representative, but will nevertheless contend that only a majoritarian two-party system can deliver strong, stable and effective leadership. Skewed, disproportional electoral results, the virtual exclusion of third and minor parties from office, and an ineffectual Parliament, are seen as acceptable, if perhaps somewhat regrettable, consequences of these supposed benefits. To insist on proportional representation, their argument goes, would leave us hostage to indecisive coalitions and unstable Governments. Worse, they say, it could cause liberal-democracy to collapse, like the Weimar Republic, since proportional representation supposedly allows dangerous extremists to erode the State.

These traditional arguments, however, are based on a fundamental misunderstanding of the nature of 'strong', 'stable' and 'effective' government. A majoritarian electoral system might guarantee a single-party Government, which can remain in office for a full term and legislate just as it pleases, but this is no guarantee of genuine strength, stability or effectiveness. Indeed, such brittle strength might well have the opposite effect; the concentration of power in an unlimited single party executive, directed by an over-powerful Prime Minister, can result in an inconsistent and knee-jerk approach to policy-making and legislation. A consensus democracy, on the other hand, is well-placed to promote good governance: the need for cooperation and compromise prevents the taking of narrow, myopic or ill-considered decisions, in favour of sensible long-term policies.

The apparent paradox of the weakness of 'strong' government was best explained by Benjamin Constant:

> Those institutions which act as barriers against power simultaneously support it. They guide it in its progress; they sustain its efforts; the moderate its excesses of violence and stimulate it in its moments of apathy. They rally around it the interests of the various classes. Even when it fights them, they impose upon it certain considerations which makes its mistakes less dangerous. But when these institutions are destroyed, power, lacking anything to contain it, begins to march haphazardly; its step becomes uneven and erratic. As it no longer follows a fixed rule, it now advances, now recoils, now becomes agitated, now restless; it never knows whether it is doing enough, or too much. Sometimes it is carried away and nothing can stop it; sometimes

it subsides and nothing can revive it. It rids itself of allies while thinking to be rid of enemies.[19]

Constant's complaint against the centralising effects of unbalanced power could easily be applied to the record of the British State since 1945. All the autonomous centres of power and authority, which, by their advice, resistance and moderating influence, helped to tame the excesses of the Westminster system, have been eroded: local government, universities, the churches, the trade unions, even the aristocracy – all have been stripped of their traditional strength, independence and identity by the centralised State and the centralised market economy. The State, instead of finding itself empowered by this lack of obstacles, instead finds itself ill-advised, unbalanced, distrusted by the public, and ultimately enfeebled.

In the absence of such traditional constraints, the two-party system becomes not only irresponsible, but positively dangerous: it puts an erratic power in the hands of one party and then, through the workings of the disproportional electoral system, transfers that power to the other party – again, with a minimum of balance and restraint. The pernicious effects of this arrangement on our public infrastructure, our social services, and our general wellbeing, are clear to see. In the space of 20 years the British steel industry was nationalised, denationalised, re-nationalised, and then privatised. Is it any wonder that the steel industry collapsed as it did? It could not withstand the perils of such a 'strong, decisive' Government.

Similarly, the economic reforms made by the Conservatives in the 1980s remain highly controversial. Even if we believe they were necessary, we must concede that they were clumsily handled. The Government had no need to appeal to moderate sentiment, nor to reconcile differences with other parties in Parliament. With its well-whipped majority, artificially reinforced by the distortions of the electoral system, Margaret Thatcher's Government could be sure of getting its all legislative plans enacted, no matter what objections the people adversely affected by them might raise.

Moreover, owing to the tendency of first-past-the-post to divide the electorate into polarised 'safe seats', it made no difference to

Thatcher whether all the people in Glasgow or Fife hated her, or only most of them. Electorally, the Government could easily afford to sustain considerable collateral damage, in the form of empty shops, destroyed communities, blighted lives and ruined chances, without fear of denting their majority. On the opposite side, the Labour Government was able to ban fox hunting without any concern for votes in rural areas. Regardless of the rights or wrongs of either issue, first-past-the-post does not translate into effective government, but into a form of government which sees little need for compromise, and can sacrifice long-term progress and stability in the rush to pursue short term, populist goals.

One imagined advantage of the majoritarian system is that it at least provides the opportunity to 'throw the rascals out'. First past the post elections are supposed to offer the electorate a direct choice between the Government and Opposition, with a consequently clear line of accountability. This is not, in fact, the case. In a consensual democracy, based on proportional representation, Governments are easier to remove from office than in majoritarian systems. In 2005 Labour managed to hold onto office with a majority of seats in the House of Commons based on 35 per cent of the votes cast, or little more than one-fourth of the total available votes, once turn-out is taken into account. It can be very difficult to throw out a Government under such circumstances: so long as the opposition is divided (that is, so long as the people desire any more meaningful say than a simple either/or choice), a Government can cling to 100 per cent of the power on a tiny fragment of the votes. With proportional representation, the 2005 general election, based on the same distribution of votes, could possibly have led to the removal from office of Tony Blair, who by then had become very unpopular. This is of course speculation, not least because proportional representation changes the way people vote (there is less need for tactical voting) as well as changing the way votes are transformed into seats, but it at least shows that the majoritarian claim to accountability lacks a basis in fact. In a consensus democracy with proportional representation, it would be easier 'to throw the rascals out'.

'All very well in theory, but what about Italy? Does it not show that proportional representation is a recipe for disaster?' This is the most common response made to any rational argument in favour of proportional representation and the consensual approach to democracy. Yet, although it is the most notorious, Italy is not the only, or even the best, example of a consensus democracy. One could just as well say, 'What about Sweden?', 'What about the Netherlands, Norway, Germany, or Denmark, or indeed any other well-governed European country?' It is true that Italy in the post-war era was unusually corrupt, unstable and ineffective, but these problems did not come from consensual democracy; they came from a combination of cultural and constitutional factors specific to Italy.[20] Since the 1990s Italy has moved towards a sort of two-party system, with a new curiously hybrid electoral system which encourages the formation of disciplined left-right blocks. Italian governments are more 'stable', in as much as one person remains in office as Prime Minister for a longer time, but are they any more effective? Are they any better at serving the public good? Some of the evidence seems to indicate that this has not been the case, and that Italy's movement towards a more majoritarian political system has made for a more authoritarian, more populist, less democratic and even less accountable form of politics.[21] Indeed, the little-learned lesson of the Italian experience might be that consensus democracy, in accordance with Constant's paradox, helps the cause of freedom and good government, even – or perhaps especially – in unfavourable social and cultural conditions.

The happy reality is that there is no trade-off between effectiveness and representativeness. A consensual democracy, based on proportional representation, a balance of power between the executive and legislature, and decentralisation, is superior on all counts. Lijphart argues, based on an extensive empirical study of 36 liberal-democracies in four continents, that consensual democracies produce better macro-economic results than majoritarian democracies. The benefits are seen not only in terms of 'hard' measures like growth, inflation and unemployment, but also in terms of 'soft' measures such as strike activity and industrial peace.[22] The need for consensus-building, for the consent of other parties and the co-operation of social partners, forces the Government to think before it acts, to justify its actions, thus reducing the risk of bad policies and increasing the likelihood of effective government for the common good.

Moreover, the policies which result from this compromise are likely to result in what Lijphart calls a 'kinder, gentler democracy', which is more humane and more ecological. Consensus democracies are less likely to put people to death, and are better at caring for the sick and the poor, than majoritarian ones.[23] They also offer a 'higher quality' of democracy, measured by the level of women's representation, political equality, turn-out, public satisfaction, levels of corruption, and degree of concordance between government policies and public opinion.[24] Policy-making in a consensual democracy is more likely to be deliberative and discursive, and to more closely approximate the civic-republican ideal of self-government. As a consequence, the sort of statesmen and stateswomen who succeed in consensus democracies are those most able to build working relationships across party lines: co-ordinators, mediators, and those with a grasp of policy issues – not ideologues or demagogues.

If we desire to create a just, humane, moderately prosperous, civic, and democratic society, all the evidence points to the need for a rather fundamental shift in our thinking. We should reconsider how we use the words 'strong', 'stable' and 'effective', learning to think of them not in terms of a single party being able to dominate Parliament in order to achieve its manifesto, but in terms of an ongoing public conversation between the Government, other parliamentary parties, local authorities, economic interests and civic society, aimed at the long-term common good. Parties will have an incentive to participate in this conversation because they will not be able to 'win' power by appealing to the interests of just one section of the population – that might win them a few seats, but they will not get into Government office unless they can co-operate with others.

The move towards a more consensual form of democracy has broad support in Scotland. The Claim of Right and the Scottish Constitutional Convention did not merely insist on self-government, but on a new form of government, intended to be more consensual, more civic, and more balanced, than the Westminster system. Accordingly, since its creation in 1999, the Scottish Parliament has been elected by proportional representation. The First Minister does not have the same all-powerful prerogatives of the Prime Minister in London. Parliament's procedures have been reformed in order to strengthen the role of Parliament in the legislative and policy-making process. Although much work remains to be done, these substantial steps towards consensus democracy must be judged a success. A period of coalition government from 1999 to 2007 meant that the Liberal Democrats were able not only to get into office, but also to contribute to legislative decision-making and carry-out important policies, such as the reform of the local government electoral system. From 2007 to 2011, the minority SNP Government gave Parliament as a whole an enhanced role. Votes were not an empty ritual or a forgone conclusion – Government proposals were amended, or even defeated, by the Scottish Parliament in a way that is starkly in contrast to Westminster norms.[b]

Political culture is 'sticky' and old habits die hard. No one would be so naïve as to suggest that Holyrood is a flawless exemplar of consensual government in action. Despite institutional reforms, many politicians still think of politics as a zero-sum game, where the aim is simply to win, if necessary by rubbishing one's opponents. The Labour Party, in particular, has yet to find its feet as a viable, principled, competent opposition. How the Scottish Parliament continues

---

[b] At the time of writing (July 2011), we are in a strange position. Westminster, despite the first-past-the-post electoral system, has a coalition Government, while Holyrood, despite proportional representation, has a single-party majority. This anomaly shows that the choice of electoral system, while important, does not guarantee any particular result. Malta, which uses a modified form of STV, has rigid two-party politics, with no third-party representation at all; Canada, which uses first-past-the-post, has a multi-party political system, with frequent minority Governments. Nevertheless, the crucial role of the electoral system cannot be denied: a proportional electoral system makes consensus democracy more likely, while a disproportional system makes it less likely.

to develop, now that one party has an unprecedented overall majority, following the May 2011 election results, remains to be seen. There is a danger that the old habits of winner-takes-all politics could become more ingrained. Even so, Scotland's experience of coalition and minority governments does confirm Lijphart's argument that there is nothing to fear, and potentially much to be gained, from seeking a more consensual approach.[25] A Constitution for Scotland should therefore make use of proportional representation and other procedural mechanisms to create a balanced, accountable and transparent political system. This means that the Prime Minister of Scotland, enjoying the confidence of the Scottish Parliament, should have the right to lead, to take the initiative and to set the direction of policy, but that all authorities should also be subject to proper scrutiny, advice, and restraint, so as to prevent corruption or the misuse of power.

# A Normal European Democracy

THE SNP'S 2002 Constitutional Policy Paper, outlining the party's vision for the constitutional future of an independent Scotland, spoke of the need to create a 'normal, democratic European nation'.[26] At a minimum, this means that Scotland's Constitution should enable the country to meet the Copenhagen criteria for EU-accession.[27] These criteria include 'stability of institutions guaranteeing democracy, the rule of law, human rights and respect for and protection of minorities'.[28]

Moreover, the idea of a 'normal' European democracy has two further implications. Firstly, it means that the Constitution of Scotland should be of a form, standard and technical quality at least equivalent to that of other leading European democracies. Secondly, it means that the quality of democracy enjoyed by the citizens of an independent Scotland, in terms of representation, participation, transparency, accountability and rights, should be at least equal to the quality of democracy enjoyed by citizens of similar European countries.[29]

The concept of a 'normal' European democracy can be contrasted against the Westminster system, which is in many ways different to the norm, and in some crucial respects inferior to the European norm. The desire to create a normal European democracy implies the rejection of the Westminster model, with its first-past-the-post elections and parliamentary sovereignty, its crown prerogatives and overbearing executive, in favour of a more 'continental' approach. An off-the-shelf Westminster-style Constitution, hastily drafted by the British Government from a dusty Colonial Office relic, would be unlikely to meet Scotland's democratic aspirations. Such a Constitution, resembling those of Jamaica or Belize, would only replicate in miniature the faults of the Westminster system, including concentration of power in the hands of the Prime Minister and a lack of checks and balances. To become independent under such an unbalanced Constitution would be a missed opportunity. It would do little more than transfer excessive power from a Prime Minister in Westminster to a similarly unrestrained Prime Minister in Holyrood, without noticeable improvement to the quality of democracy or civic life.

Rooting our constitutional desires in 'European normality' not only protects us from the dangers of excessive conservatism, introspection, and over-reliance on Westminster traditions; it is just as effective at shielding us from the opposite danger – the danger of being too radical or ambitious. If we are striving to create a normal European democracy, then utopian flights of fancy must be avoided. Our democratic imaginations might be inspired by visions of turning Edinburgh into a 21st century 'Athens of the North', but all our proposals for a workable Model Constitution must be grounded firmly in reality, and in the experience of what works in other, similar countries. It would be irresponsible to recommend an untried utopian scheme, which for all its theoretical glory would be unworkable in existing Scottish conditions.

Creating a normal European democracy in Scotland requires, then, what might be called a 'moderate-reformist' approach. Pursuing a golden mean between the unimaginative and the unrealistic, and avoiding the excesses of both conservatism and radicalism, and a moderate-reformist approach would seek to build on the progress already made in Scotland under the Scotland Act. It would accept the need for proportional representation, fixed-term Parliaments and a more balanced relationship between the executive and legislature. It would continue the trend away from Westminster practices, strengthening direct democracy, providing for constitutional entrenchment and stronger judicial review. Most of all, it would incorporate the best practices of other successful European nations, so as to produce a Scottish democracy which is more representative, more genuinely parliamentary, more consensual, accountable and decentralised.

A suitable Constitution for Scotland would therefore be similar, in overall structure, to the Constitutions of comparable 'normal European democracies', such as Ireland, Luxembourg, Iceland, Sweden, Denmark, Norway, Latvia and Estonia. Yet, in itself, this provides only a general guide. Although broadly similar in terms of principles and structures, these Constitutions differ greatly in matters of detail. The Swedish and Irish Constitutions are long and exhaustive; those of Iceland and Latvia are short and pithy. Ireland, Iceland and Latvia are parliamentary republics, with non-executive Presidents; Sweden, Norway and Luxembourg have figurehead monarchies. Ireland, Latvia and Denmark make substantial provision for referendums, which provide a potentially important popular check on the parliamentary majority; Sweden, Norway and Luxembourg make little provision for direct democracy. In Ireland, Ministers *must* be chosen from amongst the members of Parliament; in Latvia they *may* be; in Norway and Luxembourg they *may not* be. Ireland, Latvia and Luxembourg (since 1996) make robust provision for judicial review, while judicial review in Sweden, Norway and Denmark has remained quite weak. All these details can have profound effects on the operation of the Constitution and, ultimately, on the quality of democracy which the Constitution provides.

It does not end there. Every question of detail leads to another set of supplementary questions. If the Head of State is to be elected, are they to be elected by Parliament, as in Hungary and Latvia, by the people as in Ireland and Portugal, or by a special electoral college as in Germany, Italy and India? Are they to serve for just one term, or for two, or for as many as they can win? Should their term of office be four years, or five, or six? Should they have the power of pardon? If so, should they exercise it at their personal discretion, or on the advice of some advisory body? How is that other body to be created? What about the power to dissolve Parliament? Or to nominate members of the Supreme Court? The list goes on and on. It is little wonder that the usual response of common lawyers, when faced with this problem, is to throw their hands in the air and insist that it cannot be done, and that we are better off with an unwritten, make-it-up-as-you-go 'constitution'. Yet all these problems, in their manifold complexity, can be addressed. In order to address them, we need only to study the constitutional structures of other countries, to observe their practical effects, and thus to make reasonable inferences about what will work well for Scotland. These points of detail will be taken up, and illustrated by comparison to other countries, in Part Two. For now, it is necessary only explore two broad themes arising from this comparative study, which should guide our detailed constitutional choices.

The first of these themes is that the design of a good Constitution is dependent upon the application of what might be termed 'constitutional technology'. Over time, societies develop new political institutions and mechanisms to meet emerging and changing needs. Written Constitutions, the office of Ombudsman, Constitutional Courts, proportional representation, referendums and primary elections, are all examples of constitutional technologies which have been 'invented' in the past two centuries. If an innovation proves successful – that is, if it enables a better quality of liberal-democracy to be achieved, without sacrificing stability – then other countries are likely to adopt (and adapt) it. One example of this process of development and diffusion is the 'constructive vote of no-confidence'. This new constitutional device was developed in Germany after the Second World War. Its development was rooted in historical necessity: to prevent a return to the instability of the Weimar Republic, where temporary and negative coalitions of extremists and malcontents had reduced the republic to chaos. The solution, although novel, was simple: to make the removal of the Chancellor dependent upon the election of a successor by a working majority. This mechanism helps make proportional representation compatible with firm, stable leadership. It was so successful that it was copied by several other States, including Spain and Hungary.

In Europe, three 'generations' of constitutional technology can be identified. Broadly speaking, first-generation Constitutions were written between 1815 and 1918. Examples of typical first generation Constitutions include the 1831 Constitution of Belgium, the 1837 Constitution of Spain, and the 1848 *Statuto* of Piedmont-Sardinia. These early Constitutions typically featured a bicameral Parliament, with a lower chamber elected on a limited suffrage, and an upper chamber selected to represent existing social, economic and political elites. Despite enshrining the *legal* responsibility of Ministers, their impeachability by Parliament, and the need for the monarch to act upon the authority of a Ministerial counter-signature, these first generation Constitutions gave only an imperfect and indirect recognition to the principle of *political* responsibility (that is, of the need for the Government to maintain the confidence of Parliament, and to resign if it loses that confidence) which is at the heart of modern parliamentary democracy. No mention was made of votes of investiture or no-confidence. Ministers were chosen and appointed by the Monarch, who was allowed to retain a moderately active, if limited, role in politics. Few of these first generation constitutions have survived intact to the present day, and most of them have been subsequently up-dated by amendments.

The end of the First World War marked the transition to the second generation. Second-generation Constitutions are exemplified by the 1921 Constitution of Czechoslovakia, the 1922 Constitution of Latvia, the 1929 Constitution of Austria, and, of course, by the ill-fated Constitution of the Weimar Republic in Germany. These new Constitutions typically granted universal suffrage, often with proportional representation. They featured elected non-executive presidents, who in many cases took over the diminished powers of the deposed former monarchs. They also, often, incorporated certain rights and liberties into the Constitution and established constitutional courts with the power to annul laws on the grounds of unconstitutionality. In this respect, Austria and Czechoslovakia were pioneers. New constitutional devices providing for direct democracy, such as referendums and popular initiatives, also began to take root in this period.

The third generation of constitutional development in Europe began after the Second World War. It was a response to the collapse of liberal-democracy across most of newly-democratised Europe in the 1930s. The third generation is best represented by the Basic Law of the Federal Republic of Germany, which corrected the perceived faults of the Weimar Constitution. Proportional representation was retained, but a threshold was introduced to prevent fragmentation amongst a plethora of small and antagonistic parties. The powers of the President were reduced, and the Government placed on an explicitly parliamentary basis. Crucially, the relationship between the Head of State, the Government and Parliament, which in first and second generation Constitutions had been largely based on expedient custom, was rationalised and written into the Constitution.

Some third generation Constitutions also saw the introduction of ancillary mechanisms designed to control and constrain parliamentary majorities. These mechanisms recognise the fact that the Government's political responsibility to Parliament is not, in itself, a sufficient guarantee of good governance. When the Government is supported by a disciplined majority in Parliament, additional checks and balances, from outside the parliamentary system, must be developed in order to limit the abuse of power, prevent excessive patronage, ensure the non-manipulability of the law and guarantee accountability and transparency. The Constitution of Spain, adopted in 1978, is an excellent example of a sophisticated third generation Constitution. It includes a *Defensor del Pueblo* (Ombudsman) to protect the people against maladministration, *Tribunal de Cuentas* (Court of Accounts) to ensure financial probity and accountability, and a *Consejo General del Poder Judicial* (General Council of the Judicial Power) to control judicial appointments and uphold judicial independence.

If democracy is to survive, it appears we might soon have to develop a fourth generation of constitutional technology. The source for this technology might come from a rediscovery of mechanisms from ancient and medieval republics, not least the use of random lot, rotation in office, and town-square democracy. The effect would be to challenge the primacy of party representation and restore important elements of genuine self-government by the community. However, none of this is yet established; if we desire to create a workable and well-proven Constitution for Scotland, then we must, for the time being, file these ideas away in the 'wait and see' box. In the meantime, our aim should be to establish a solid, reliable, third generation Constitution, at least equal to those of the rest of Europe.

Scotland has an advantage of being a 'late adopter' of constitutional technology; there are many other countries from which we can learn the 'dos' and 'don'ts'. Writing a good, workable, 'third-generation' Constitution for Scotland is not, therefore, a leap into the unknown, as some defenders of the status quo might claim. Rather, it is an act of consolidation, which seeks to adapt well-tried and tested constitutional technologies to Scotland's situation.

The second theme to emerge from the comparative study of other Constitutions is that there are many ways to achieve similar aims. In Germany, protection against the abuse of power by the governing majority is secured by means of a strong upper chamber, federalism, and an active Constitutional Court; the German President is a weak, indirectly elected figurehead, and there is no scope for referendums on the federal level. In Ireland, the referendum and the ability of the President to refer dubious legislation to the Supreme Court serve this purpose: the Senate is a weak, almost useless, body. In Denmark, which has no second chamber, no President, and only weak judicial review, the main check against the abuse of power is a preference for minority governments, coupled with a strong opposition that can appeal to the people by means of referendums triggered by the parliamentary minority.

Here we see the importance of balance. Having too many checking institutions is almost as dangerous as having too few. A State which adopted all of the constitutional contrivances discussed above could descend into deadlock and paralysis, and its democratic system, unable to cope with the push and pull of demands placed upon it, could collapse at the hands of a populist demagogue (this partly explains what happened to the Weimar Republic). Whether we choose to have a President armed with a power of referral, a strong second chamber, or some sort of minority-veto referendum mechanism, is largely a question of preference, history, and practicality, not of fundamental principle. What matters is that we find a way (any appropriate, workable way) to ensure that Parliament is representative of and responsible to the people, and that the Government is properly accountable to Parliament, so that together they can govern for the common good, whilst also being restrained, as far as possible, from invading our liberties, and from using power in selfish or corrupt ways.

The Model Constitution presented in this book liberally borrows, in content, style, and basic structure, from the text prepared for the SNP by Neil MacCormick. This draft was first produced in 1977 and most recently re-released, with minor modifications, in 2002.[30] The MacCormick draft is in many ways an inspiring document. It is a 'moderate-reformist' text, which envisages a parliamentary, consensual and decentralised Scottish State. It provides for a unicameral Parliament elected by proportional representation. Parliament would be elected for fixed four-year terms, subject only to premature dissolution by the Head of State in the event of being unable to form of a Government. As a substitute for the delaying and revising power of a second chamber, a minority-veto and referendum mechanism is proposed. The monarchy would be retained, although the Crown prerogatives would be somewhat curtailed, with powers of peace, war and treaty-making transferred to Parliament, and the conventional relationship between the Head of State and the executive placed upon a less ambiguous constitutional basis: the Prime Minister would be formally elected by and responsible to Parliament. There would be an independent judiciary chosen on the advice of a non-partisan appointments committee, and provision for autonomous local self-government within the framework of a unitary but decentralised State. The MacCormick draft would also guarantee protection for basic civil, legal, religious, and political rights, based on the European Convention on Human Rights and its protocols. All this would be embodied in a rigid Constitution, capable of amendment only by a super majority of Parliament, followed by a referendum. In all of these resects the Model Constitution closely follows the MacCormick draft.

However, the MacCormick draft is far from perfect, and needs some careful revision. It makes no provision for an Ombudsman, Auditor-General, or other instruments of redress, scrutiny and accountability. The electoral system is poorly specified, and there is no Electoral Commission to protect Parliament from gerrymandering by the majority party. Its provisions concerning parliamentary privileges and procedures are sketchy at best. It fails to take into account the developments already made in the organisation of the Scottish Parliament since devolution, such as the creation of the Parliamentary Bureau and the Parliamentary Corporate Body. Crucially, it does not adequately distinguish between the roles of the Prime Minister and the Head of State, and treats certain royal prerogatives – such as that of refusing assent to legislation – in a way which is unclear and potentially problematic.

Owing to these omissions and ambiguities, the MacCormick draft does not meet Scotland's highest aspirations for democratic reform, and falls somewhat short of contemporary European best practice. These criticisms in points of detail are not intended to denigrate the excellent work done by Neil MacCormick and others. Rather, their purpose is simply to show that the MacCormick draft, although very good in essence, and an excellent starting-point, would benefit from close scrutiny and careful revision. The Model Constitution therefore re-works the MacCormick draft on the micro-level, whilst broadly accepting its macro-level and meso-level choices. In other words, it closes the loopholes of the MacCormick text, and improves it in many small but important matters of detail, without diverging from it in matters of general principle or basic structure. As such, the Model Constitution remains faithful to the SNP's long-standing constitutional policy, but also incorporates lessons learned from the Scotland Act, and from the Constitutions of other European (and, to a lesser extent, British Commonwealth) democracies.

PART TWO

# Explanatory Notes

SO FAR, THIS BOOK has discussed the main principles of a Constitution for Scotland, and has sought to identify, in broad outline, the most viable and acceptable constitutional forms for an independent Scottish state. The second half of this book, presented as a set of explanatory notes to the text of the proposed Model Constitution, goes on to apply these principles, and to build on these basic constitutional forms. It discusses each of the major institutions of the Model Constitution in turn, explaining the reasons why certain specific constitutional proposals have been recommended. It must be stressed, once more, that these recommendations are not intended to be the final word on the subject, nor is any claim made for the perfection of the Model Constitution – the author's aim is simply to present the Model Constitution an example of what a good Constitution for Scotland might look like, and perhaps to set it up as a starting point for further debate.

## Preliminaries

The first Article of the Model Constitution, entitled 'Preliminaries' sets out the foundations of the Scottish State. It opens with a statement of basic principles – a declaration of what sort of country Scotland aspires to be:

> Scotland is a free, sovereign and independent commonwealth.
> Its form of government is a parliamentary democracy based upon the sovereignty of the people, social justice, solidarity and respect for human rights.

In addition to 'parliamentary democracy', 'sovereignty of the people' and 'respect for human rights', a strong commitment to 'social justice' and 'solidarity' – a sense of 'all being in it together' – is fundamental to the moral vision of an independent Scotland. This is deeply rooted in Scotland's self-identity and character. Despite gross and persistent material inequalities, Scotland boasts an egalitarian ethos and communal values. The Thatcherite claim that 'there is no such thing as society' was, according to Kenny MacAskill MSP (SNP), treated as a sort of 'heresy':

Scotland [...] is most certainly an egalitarian country. It has been forged on an anvil of historical events that have created a culture of equality and of public service. From the days of the Reformation and the creation of parish schools there has been a drive to educate all and for all to participate.

Whether in the urbanised central belt or the rural crofting counties, communities grew up seeing the need for co-operation, whether against the excesses of the landlord or the industrialist.[31]

These egalitarian, fraternal values are well expressed by Scotland's national poet, Robert Burns. Where else, but in a country which invented universal public education, where farm hands could go to university, and where John Knox took it upon himself to admonish Queen Mary, could a Parliament be opened with these scything, pretence-deflating, words?

'Ye see yon birkie, ca'd a lord,
Wha struts, an' stares, an' a' that;
Tho' hundreds worship at his word,
He's but a coof for a' that:
For a' that, an' a' that,
His ribband, star, an' a' that:
The man o' independent mind
He looks an' laughs at a' that.'[32]

Of course, the practical meaning and importance these declaratory expressions will have to be worked out by future generations of Scottish citizens. The foundational values of the Scottish State will have to be contested, explored, and re-applied in different times and circumstances. Their interpretation and application will doubtless vary in accordance with the ideological orientation of successive Governments. Nevertheless, to state these values and principles clearly (much as the French Constitution declares its allegiance to 'liberty, equality, fraternity') will at least place them at the centre of our political life, and establish them as a common, basic, point of reference. They are a reminder that we should not let politicians win power for selfish and partisan ends, but rather should insist that 'all things be done for edification' (i.e. for the building-up of the 'commonwealth'). The word 'commonwealth', in this context, is intended simply as a translation of the Latin term 'res publica' – a self-governing comm-unity existing for the service of the common good ('common-weal').

The remainder of this preliminary article requires little further explanation. Section 2 establishes the principle, discussed at length in the first part of this book, of constitutional supremacy over ordinary Acts of Parliament. Section 3 marks our Scotland's territory and lays claim to territorial waters. Section 4 defines Scottish citizenship, which is based on the principle of residence: everyone domiciled in Scotland at the time of the promulgation of the Constitution shall be entitled to Scottish citizenship. Thereafter, Parliament may legislate for the acquisition of citizenship by birth, marriage or naturalisa-tion, and for the loss or renunciation of citizenship. This reflects an open, civic and democratic, rather than a narrow and ethnic, under-standing of Scottish nationhood. To be Scottish is not to have 'Scottish blood' – there is no such thing. It is not even necessary to have been born in Scotland, only to be domiciled in Scotland, and to share in a covenant of commitment to Scotland, to its laws and civil institutions, and to the well-being of one's fellow-citizens. Finally, Section 5 establishes universal adult suffrage, in accordance with the usual requirements of liberal-democracy, subject only to such reasonable exemptions as may be applied by law for convicted criminals serving a sentence and for those who are certified as mentally incapable.

## Head of State

Whether an independent Scotland should retain or abolish the monarchy is a question of largely symbolic, rather than practical, importance. If the Constitution is well designed in all other respects, it may work just as well with an elected or hereditary Head of State. However, symbols are too important to ignore: they are the keys to legitimacy and acceptability, and are central to the relationship between the State and the people it serves.

A significant number of Scottish people would undoubtedly welcome a republic. This, however, would run the unacceptable risk of alienating those – perhaps the majority – who retain a visceral loyalty to the Crown, or at least a residual loyalty to the present

Queen. After a potentially close and divisive campaign for independence, the Scottish State must move quickly to reconcile persons of conservative and unionist sentiments to the reality of independent Statehood. As the SNP realise, keeping the Queen, as a symbolic link with a shared British past and with the rest of the Commonwealth, is the best way to achieve this reconciliation. The retention of the monarchy will ease transitional tensions by reassuring unionists, particularly those of the older generation, that the 'social union' remains intact, and that independence need not be a threat to their British identity. After all, many Scots have for three centuries maintained a cultural identity which is both 'Scottish and British' within the political framework of the United Kingdom; there is no reason why people could not continue, through the shared symbols of monarchy, to maintain a 'Scottish and British' identity within the political framework of an independent Scotland.

A continuation of the monarchy is therefore the best initial choice for Scotland, and a republican solution should, for the time being, be set aside (although, of course, the question might be re-opened in the future, when it could be dealt with by a simple constitutional amendment). This does not mean, however, that the monarchy of an independent Scotland should necessarily duplicate, either in form or function, the British monarchy. The retention the Queen as Head of State does not require the perpetuation of Crown prerogative powers, nor the continued 'pomp and circumstance' of the British monarchy. It is possible, in the words of Viscount Vilain, speaking at the Belgian Constituent Assembly in 1831, to be in favour of a constitutional monarchy, 'founded on the most liberal, the most popular and the most republican principles'.[33] This section will therefore sketch out a vision for a modern, democratic monarchy, which would best meet the needs and aspirations of an independent Scotland.

The first point to make is that the monarchy of Scotland should be established only as a symbolic 'cherry' on top of a resolutely democratic constitutional cake. This approach obviously rejects all 'divine right' theories of monarchy, as well as all claims based solely on privilege. The monarch would not, even in theory, possess governing powers, but would serve only as a ceremonial and civic representative of the people, holding a constitutional office, with narrowly defined responsibilities and duties.

Here it is necessary to distinguish between the monarch and the Crown. The Crown is the central legal-political institution of the British State, the undying office through which executive power is exercised. The monarch is the person who, by hereditary succession, occupies the Crown. It is not the symbolism of the monarch, but the great and unaccountable power of the Crown, which is a danger to democracy. In the British State, this power is exercised in practice by the Prime Minister. The Prime Minister, under the cover and shadow of the Crown, is able to exercise extensive prerogative power over matters such as the appointment of Lords and judges, the granting of honours and the declaration of war. This enables the Government to act in an autocratic manner, and to shield itself from scrutiny and accountability.

Clarity, transparency and accountability – virtues by which the new Scottish democracy should seek to define itself – all require that powers be held by those who are actually to exercise them, and that the bounds and limitations of power be known and fixed. In this respect, the British custom of vesting the whole executive power in the Crown, to be exercised on the 'advice' of Ministers, is inadequate. It is not only misleading and fictitious, but also deeply ambiguous. It is not clear, because it is nowhere stated, or written down, exactly what the bounds of monarchical authority are. It is widely accepted that, in certain very rare circumstances, the Queen may exercise a personal choice of Prime Minister, or choose to grant or withhold a dissolution of Parliament, or even, perhaps, to cross the constitutional Rubicon by withholding assent to legislation. Yet we do not know what these circumstances are, nor are we told how or why such decisions would be made. It is not clear which of these reserve powers have fallen into disuse, or which of them could be rapidly revived. The result is a web of confusion.

Moreover, these uncertain and ill-defined reserve powers can lead us into a false sense of security. Many believe that the monarchy is a guardian-of-last-resort, to protect us from the danger of tyranny – but it is difficult to see how such a check could operate, when its powers are so uncertain and their legitimacy rests on such a fragile base.

The Constitutions of Spain (1978) and Sweden (1974) are the best examples of modern Constitutions that combine civic democracy with a figurehead monarchy. In both cases, executive powers are entrusted directly and unequivocally to the Government. The Head of State is left with only a limited range of non-executive functions, which are clearly stated and defined. This removes the mystique of power and makes the role of the Head of State clearer and more in keeping with democratic principles. If we are to retain the monarchy in Scotland, it is to these examples, and not to the British or Commonwealth tradition, that we must look for answers.

The Model Constitution therefore keeps the hereditary monarchy as a symbolic figurehead, but abolishes the Crown as a political and legal institution. The powers and prerogatives formerly belonging to the Crown are transferred to the Government (with the exception of those which are abolished, or are transferred to other institutions, such as Parliament, the Presiding Officer, or the Judicial Council). This reform has already been anticipated, to some extent, by the Scotland Act of 1998. Under that Act, executive powers in Scotland are vested not in 'the Crown' but in 'the Scottish Ministers', while certain delicate constitutional powers, such as the nomination of the First Minister and the dissolution of Parliament, are in fact exercised by a parliamentary vote, or by the Presiding Officer. Although some might shudder at the thought of this 'radicalism', the Model Constitution would simply extend and clarify an existing trend, and bring Scotland into line with the best of modern European Constitutions.

The ceremonial duties of a democratic monarchy would encompass those official functions where the authority of the State, rather than that of the Government of the day, is paramount. This might include acting as commander-of-chief of the armed forces, awarding honours in the name of the people, and accrediting and receiving ambassadors. A permanent and non-partisan Head of State can perform these duties with greater dignity, authority and solemnity, than a Prime Minister, since the latter's public standing will necessarily be compromised by party politics and by the daily business of governing. In these cases, the Head of State has no personal or discretionary power. The royal sceptre is, and ought to be, a merely passive and formal instrument; it merely embodies the authority of the State, and gives legitimacy to others – chiefly to the Prime Minister.

The civic functions of the Head of State are broader, and allow wider scope for personal discretion. Under this heading come all those actions by which the Head of State promotes the country in cultural and social spheres, encourages virtuous citizenship and charitable works, articulates the values and aspirations of the people, and promotes public ethics. This civic function is vitally important: in the absence of moral leadership and a strong personal example, the civic values which sustain freedom are likely to be eroded by our selfish concerns and by the short-term thinking of politicians. No other institution can perform this civic function as well, or with as much authority, as an independent, non-executive Head of State: Parliament and the Government are burdened and compromised by the demands of day-to-day activity. As the then President of Ireland, Mary Robinson, put it an interview with US journalist Charles Rose in 1994:

> [The Irish Presidency] gives an opportunity to represent in a different way, in a way that is complementary to the role played by government... ...its strength lies in the fact that it is not involved in day-to-day political policy-making, so it is possible to look at things in a slightly different way, from a longer perspective; to perhaps try to influence trends, try to promote and identify values which are important; touch a different chord with people.[34]

Whether this civic function is better performed by a hereditary or an elected Head of State is a matter for debate. When royalty represents a foreign dynasty, or has been discredited in the eyes of the people by its association with forces of reaction and oppression, the only available course of action is to abolish the monarchy and to institute an elected President. It would have been impracticable, for example, for the newly independent Czechoslovakia to have adopted the Hapsburg monarchy after 1918. On the other hand, where the monarch is respected and treasured by the people, and is felt by the majority of the people to reflect and embody their values and aspirations, the hereditary system need not necessarily be an obstacle to civic, democratic virtues. Indeed, the hereditary system might even be an advantage, in as much as it avoids the party-politics associated with elections, and can tap into the seam of a nation's history and mythology.

Alongside these ceremonial and civic functions, Heads of State in many parliamentary democracies also serve a third, 'constitutional' or 'moderating', function: they are required to act as a constitutional arbiter, as a counterpoise to the active governing powers, and as a guarantor of the constitutional functioning of all other public institutions. It is in this capacity that a Head of State might, for example, have the authority to dissolve Parliament and call new elections in certain circumstances, or to refuse assent to legislation that is deemed unconstitutional, or to make certain appointments to institutions – such as Electoral Commissions – which are intended to be independent of the government of the day.

Here the elective and hereditary models differ. An elected Head of State usually has the capacity, and the democratic legitimacy, to exercise these moderating powers. For example, in 2011 the President of Latvia exercised his constitutional power to call a referendum on the dissolution of Parliament, while the President of Iceland has, since the financial crisis of 2008, twice referred controversial legislation to the people. It is usually deemed inappropriate, however, to entrust such powers to a hereditary monarch – who lacks any democratic mandate and is unaccountable for their proper exercise. In consequence, the powers of the monarchy tend to atrophy, and the vacuum is filled by an increase in the powers of the Prime Minister. Thus, for example, in the United Kingdom the dissolution of Parliament has ceased to be a royal prerogative, and has become, in effect, a Prime Ministerial pre-rogative. In other words, the problem with a hereditary monarchy in a parliamentary democracy is not that it makes the Head of State too powerful, but rather that it makes the Head of State too weak, and thereby allows the Prime Minister to be too powerful, at the expense of the balancing powers.

One solution, pioneered by Sweden, is to separate the ceremonial and civic functions of the Head of State from the moderating functions, and to vest the latter in another institution. For example, in Sweden the Prime Minister is formally nominated not by the King, but by the Speaker (Presiding Officer) of Parliament, while the polite fiction of 'royal assent' has been replaced by the scrutiny of legislation by the 'Law Council', which scrutinises proposed laws for their conformity to the Constitution.

Following the Swedish example, and also the practice of Scotland under the Scotland Act, the Model Constitution gives the Presiding Officer two moderating powers of great importance. Firstly, the Presiding Officer has to decide on the premature dissolution of Parliament (under certain defined conditions, if a government cannot be formed). Secondly, he or she may refer legislation to the Supreme Court for an advisory ruling on its constitutionality before enactment. It is expected that these two powers will be used rarely and sparingly, but, if they are to be used at all, they are better placed in the hands of the Presiding Officer than in those of a hereditary monarch – or, for that matter, than in those of the Prime Minister. The Presiding Officer, being an elected official of Parliament, but somewhat removed from the party-political fray, is exactly the sort of person to whom these delicate moderating powers can be safely entrusted. The Head of State may exercise other constitutional or moderating powers on the binding advice of other institutions; judges, for example, would be appointed on the advice of an independent Judicial Appointments Council.

Having considered the monarch's functions and duties, it remains to discuss the changes of style that would bring a more democratic touch to the monarchy. These are matters of practice rather than constitutional law, and are not directly mentioned in the text of the Model Constitution.

Firstly, the monarch should never be referred to as 'the Sovereign'. Sovereignty should never reside in a person, but only in the people – that is, in the 'whole community of the realm'. Secondly, the ancient title of 'Queen (or King) of Scots', implying consensual chieftainship rather than absolute royalty, should be restored to official use, as should the ancient, somewhat more egalitarian, form of address ('Your Grace', rather than 'Your Majesty'). These points, while stylistic rather than substantive, are necessary in order to symbolically underline historical continuity with the pre-Union Kingdom of Scots.

Scotland would pay for its own civil list out of the Scottish treasury to support the Queen of Scots in her role in Scotland. This should be kept with moderate levels, and never used to subsidise the revenues of the royal household in London. There would also have to be some changes in court ritual. The aim is that the Head of State should be maintained in befitting dignity, but never extravagance; they should be respected, but never adulated or bowed down to. Excessive regard to particular persons is out of keeping with a civic and democratic culture, and jars against the strong egalitarianism and simplicity of Scotland's Reformed tradition. In London, the Queen might ride in an eighteenth century gilded coach; but in Edinburgh, as Queen of Scots, she would be well-advised to adopt the low-key and unpretentious style of a Scandinavian 'bicycling monarchy'.

As long as the personal union between the two monarchies endures, we must deal with the problem of absenteeism. The monarch is unlikely to live in Scotland all year round, and would have to delegate his or her duties during long periods of absence. For this reason, the proposed Model Constitution provides for the appointment of a Lord High Commissioner, who would serve 'in loco regis', acting as the official representative of the Head of State in Scotland. The use of the title 'Lord High Commissioner', rather than the more conventional 'Governor-General', as found in other Commonwealth realms, is a point of stylistic importance; it represents the fact that Scotland is not an ex-colony of the United Kingdom, nor a mere cut from the Westminster bough; it is a free, separate and equal kingdom, having parity with England. The office of Lord High Commissioner has, since the Union of 1707, existed only in connection with the Church of Scotland, as the monarch's representative to the General Assembly. The Model Constitution would extend the Lord High Commissioner's duties to include deputising for the monarch's secular, as well as ecclesiastical, functions. In order to ensure that the Lord High Commissioner is a person above the fray of party-politics, and remains sufficiently independent from the Government of the day, the Model Constitution prescribes that the appointments to this office should be made on a bi-partisan basis, after consultation with the Prime Minister and the Leader of the Opposition.[c]

## Parliament

The central institution of a parliamentary democracy is, of course, the Parliament itself. Parliament selects the Government and holds it to account, it enacts laws and ratifies treaties, and serves as the deliberative assembly of the nation. Getting Parliament right matters. If Parliament is defective, the political system as a whole will be defective; if it is weak, then the executive will not be properly scrutinised or held to account, and the public good will suffer; if it is corrupt, the whole polity will be corrupt; if it is unrepresentative, the interests of the people not be properly served.

As noted in the first part, proportional representation is required in order to ensure that Parliament is properly representative, to encourage coalition governments, and to help preserve a working balance of power between the executive and legislature. However, there are many different forms of proportional representation, and the form chosen has important political consequences. It will determine the effective threshold of votes a party requires in order to win representation, the degree of proportionality between votes cast and

---

[c] It is possible, of course, that an independent Scotland might, at some future point, choose to alter the line or order of succession, thereby separating the Scots Crown from that of England (in much the same way as that of Luxembourg was separated from that of the Netherlands).

seats received, and the extent of infra-party and inter-party competition (i.e. the degree to which the elector can express a choice between individual candidates or just between fixed party lists).

There is no scholarly consensus about which form of proportional representation is objectively 'the best'. What matters most, however, is not that we have the 'best' system, but that an adequate system is clearly specified in the Constitution. In the absence of detailed specification, the governing majority could potentially manipulate the electoral rules to its own partisan advantage. Such myopic and partisan manipulation of the electoral system could damage the legitimacy of the electoral process.

The Model Constitution, in order to provide the necessary certainty, and to reduce the risk of partisan manipulation, prescribes the electoral system in some detail. This means, however, that we are forced to decide in favour of one particular system to the exclusion of all others. This is a difficult and controversial decision, since both the Single Transferable Vote (STV) and Mixed-Member Proportional (MMP) systems have their respective supporters, each of whom have valid and deeply-held reasons for their preference. The SNP's own position on this question has varied. In 1997, an MMP system was preferred, while in 2002 official policy was in favour of the STV.[35] The Model Constitution opts for the MMP system chiefly because it has the advantage of restricting intra-party choices. This encourages both voters and candidates to focus their attention on national policy issues, rather than on the sort of hyper-local client-centred politics that flourishes, in countries like Ireland and Malta, under STV. MMP, on the other hand, is tried and tested in Scotland, and would, at least for the interim, enable the existing electoral system established by the Scotland Act 1998 to continue in being, thus reducing the difficulties of transition.

The proportionality of a MMP system depends upon the number of regional list seats in proportion to the number of constituency seats, and on the 'district magnitude' of the regions (the average number of members elected from each region list).[36] The Model Constitution therefore prescribes that at least 40 per cent of the members of

Parliament be elected from regional lists, and that the number elected from each regional list be at least seven. Again, what matters is not such much that we arrive at the perfect specification, but that we impose clear rules, and thereby remove the risk of manipulation by incumbent majorities. The Model Constitution, for the avoidance of doubt, specifies that the number of members to be elected from each constituency must be determined in proportion to its share of the population.

Proportionality also depends on thresholds – that is, the minimum share of the vote necessary to win sits. To avoid the potential raising of high artificial thresholds by incumbent parties, the Model Constitution states that an artificial threshold for the distribution of regional list seats, if applied, should not exceed four per cent nationally. This maximum permitted threshold, derived from Sweden's example, would be sufficient to prevent excessive fragmentation of the party system, with its inherent risks of instability, while still enabling a broad range of views to be represented.

Parliament should always be large enough, in terms of the number of its members, to be broad, inclusive, and truly representative, but not so large as to make orderly debate impossible. The Model Constitution thus prescribes that Parliament must always have at least 120 members. It could consist of a greater number if so determined by the electoral law, up to a maximum of 200. The current size of the Scottish Parliament, 129 members, remains a reasonable default size.

There is a strong case for fixed-term Parliaments. At Westminster, the prerogative power of the Prime Minister to dissolve Parliament (i.e. the expectation that the Queen acts on the Prime Minister's advice in such matters) has traditionally given the governing party an electoral advantage, in choosing the date of the election to suit the rising and falling of the opinion polls. It also serves as an instrument for enforcing the dominance of the Government over Parliament, as the Prime Minister can use the threat of dissolution to keep independent-minded back-benchers in line. Ultimately, the power of dissolution-at-will means that Parliament remains in being only as long as the Government pleases. This means that the House of Commons cannot exercise its power to remove a Prime Minister from office by means of a vote of no-confidence, without thereby running the very serious risk of triggering a general election and potentially causing many members to lose their seats.[37]

The notion of a 'fixed term' does not mean, however, that there is no possibility of an early dissolution. In a parliamentary system, the absolute prohibition of early dissolution could be problematic – if Parliament were unable to agree on the appointment of a Prime Minister, for example, or if a deep political crisis were to occur which only a fresh appeal to the people could resolve. There must then, even with 'fixed terms', be a measure of flexibility. The crucial point is that Prime Minister, or the Government, should not have a free hand in the decision of whether, and when, to dissolve Parliament. These decisions should be taken, within more or less narrow rules, by an impartial 'arbitrator' or by a decision of Parliament.

MacCormick's draft Constitution therefore allows the Head of State to dissolve Parliament if a Prime Minister cannot be appointed within a reasonable time following a general election, or following the resignation or removal of the former Prime Minister. Dissolution in such situations is sometimes necessary – at the very least, the threat of dissolution can help to concentrate the minds of parliamentarians on the importance of finding a Prime Minister acceptable to the majority.

The Model Constitution incorporates this rule from the MacCormick draft, with two slight modifications. Firstly, it would be invoked on the advice of the Presiding Officer, who would be in a good position to exercise this delicate power with discretion and an assumption of neutrality, while allowing the Head of State to continue in a purely representative capacity, free from political controversy. Secondly, clear time-limits would be set – a dissolution under this rule would be possible only if a Prime Minister has not been elected within a period of 30 days after a general election, or within 30 days after the death, removal or resignation of the former incumbent Prime Minister.

In addition, the Model Constitution requires the Presiding Officer to dissolve Parliament if so demanded by a resolution passed by a two-thirds majority of Parliament. This would provide a clear, legitimate and above-board way for Parliament to resolve an intransient deadlock or to seek a new mandate from the people, but would transfer the decision from the Prime Minister to Parliament. Together, these rules mirror the provisions of the 1998 Scotland Act, and in this respect the Model Constitution proposes little more than the codification and entrenchment of existing practice.

Subject to these provisions concerning dissolution, a four-year parliamentary term is recommended. The relevant principle is that shorter terms of office keep parliamentarians in closer touch with the public, but at the expense of more frequent electioneering and a possible lack of long-term stability, while longer terms provide greater stability, but at the expense of allowing politicians to drift away from the people. On the one hand, it is important that those who are elected to Parliament have the opportunity to carry out and see through a consistent policy; on the other hand, it is also important that the people should be able to rectify bad choices at frequent intervals, and remove from office those who have shown themselves to be unworthy of public confidence. A term of four years (which is usual in the Parliaments in most other European democracies, although some have five-year terms) would be appropriate.

An extension of Parliament's term, for up to one year, would also be permitted, in time of war or grave public emergency, by the authority of a two-thirds majority vote of Parliament. This would allow some additional flexibility, in cases where it is impossible or impractical to hold a general election, whilst also providing a safeguard against the abuse of this power.

The Constitution should also lay down basic rules concerning the way in which Parliament organises itself and conducts its business. These details of procedure can greatly affect the autonomy of Parliament and the role of the opposition and of committees, and hence determine the ability of Parliament to effectively influence legislation and control the executive.

At Westminster, the organisation and operations of Parliament are skewed in favour of the Government. The prevailing assumption is that Parliament works for the Government – its function is to expedite the transaction of Government business with a minimum of fuss. The Scotland Act, in an effort to strike a healthy balance of power between the Scottish Parliament and Government, rejected the Westminster system in favour of a more active and participatory Parliament. Greater protection is given, both in the Scotland Act itself and in the Standing Orders of the Scottish Parliament, to the rights of the opposition and of minorities. The Scottish Parliament is able to determine its own order of business – with due regard for the needs of both Government and other parties – acting through a Parliamentary Bureau on which all parties are represented. Meanwhile, Parliament's administrative functions (such as the upkeep of its buildings, security, employment of clerical staff, and so forth) are performed by a non-partisan Parliamentary Corporate body. In these respects, the Model Constitution follows the provisions of the Scotland Act and the practices of the Scottish Parliament. Indeed, it would go further than the Scotland Act in protecting the rights of the opposition, minorities and of backbenches. Certain important and sensitive decisions, such as expelling a member for misbehaviour, and amending the Standing Orders of Parliament, would have to be decided by a two-thirds majority vote. Also, to ensure that the opposition and private members have the chance to contribute to the policy agenda and properly hold the Government to account, they would be guaranteed at least a fourth of parliamentary time.

According to the Model Constitution, the Presiding Officer would be chosen by Parliament after each general election, and the convention that they are to act in a non-partisan manner would, for the avoidance of doubt, be specified in the text of the Constitution. The Presiding Officer would preside over the Parliamentary Bureau and the Corporate Body, and would also have the authority to call Parliament into an emergency session if requested by one-third of its members, or by the Government.

The process laid down by the Model Constitution for the enactment of laws is loosely based on that of the devolved Scottish

Parliament. There are three stages: firstly, a plenary debate on the general principles and aims of the bill; secondly, detailed examination of the bill in committee; thirdly, a full debate on the bill and any proposed amendments, leading to a final vote. The Model Constitution does, however, propose some major reforms to this legislative process. These reforms are intended to improve the quality of legislation, to increase scope for democratic contestability, and to prevent the passage of selfish, hurried or ill-considered legislation.

The first proposed reform is that bills should be capable of being introduced by means of a pubic petition signed by at least five per cent of the voters. This would provide a way for ordinary members of the public who feel strongly about particular issues to give voice to their concerns and to place their proposals on Parliament's agenda. This would also enable issues that do not fit neatly into party lines to be addressed and debated in a slightly less partisan atmosphere (because members of Parliament debating such a proposal would not necessarily be arguing for or against the Government). Of course, getting an issue on the agenda and being able to introduce a bill is no guarantee that the bill will pass – that decision still rests solely with Parliament – but it at least guarantees that people can get a fair hearing, and have a chance to make their case in Parliament on issues important to them. It might mean that issues that would otherwise fester are brought to light and addressed.

The addition of a 'minority-veto referendum' mechanism is the second proposed change to the legislative process. Under this mechanism, two-fifths of the members of Parliament (i.e. 40 per cent of the total membership) may demand that any bill (other than a money bill or a bill that is certified as urgent by the unanimous decision of the Parliamentary Bureau), be suspended for at least 12 months. After this period of suspension has elapsed, the bill may be put to the vote again in Parliament, with or without amendment, and may be passed by absolute majority vote. During the period of suspension, however, the Government may decide to override the suspensive veto by putting the bill to the people in a referendum. If the bill is approved by a majority of those voting in the referendum, it is at once presented for royal assent; if not, it is deemed to have been rejected.

This minority-veto referendum mechanism, which is substantially similar to that proposed by Neil MacCormick and endorsed by the SNP's 2002 constitutional policy statement,[38] is intended to act as a check on the excessive power of the majority. While appearing to draw on similar provisions in the Constitutions of Denmark, Iceland, Latvia and Ireland, the specific details of this proposal are unique. It is not intended to result in frequent referendums, but rather to compensate for the lack of a second chamber's powers of revision and delay; it encourages the Government to avoid the risk of a frustrating delay or embarrassing referendum defeat by taking the opposition's objections and proposed amendments seriously.

Nevertheless, the Government would still be in a strong position. These rules are the minimum necessary to prevent outright domination by the majority of the day; they would in no way hinder stable governance or effective law-making. Faced with a two-fifths minority who are strongly opposed to a bill, the Government would, in effect, have three options: if the Government is in a hurry, in no mood to compromise with the minority, and confident of popular approval, the Government might choose to put the bill to a referendum; if the Government thinks it prudent to defer the issue for 12 to 18 months, and then re-present the bill, perhaps with some subtle amendments, then this option is still available. If, on the other hand, the Government wishes neither to wait for so long, nor to risk a referendum, it can negotiate with the opposition parties in the hope of persuading them to refrain from invoking this mechanism.

Requiring two-fifths of the members of Parliament to initiate the minority-veto referendum procedure ensures that it is unlikely to be invoked except at the instigation of the Leader of the Opposition. Minor parties and independents will not, under most foreseeable circumstances, be able to use it as a means of disruption or attention-seeking – at least not unless they can band together to form a substantial opposition bloc. It is not in the interests of the Leader of the Opposition to abuse this mechanism, since the Government could call his or her bluff by putting the bill to the people, and no party will wish to risk undermining its creditability, and depleting its electoral funds, by provoking referendums on bills of minor importance. So referendums are likely to be called only when the severity of political division requires it – in which circumstances, they may prove to be an excellent way of focusing, and then defusing, political tension. Moreover, the Model Constitution prohibits any member of Parliament from invoking this mechanism more than three times during any one session of Parliament – a rule which encourages them to think carefully before making use of it, so as to 'keep their powder dry'.

Overall, this procedure provides an excellent balance, which should encourage a moderate and mature form of democracy. The minority-veto referendum system would be an effective remedy against attempts by the majority to impose divisive, hurried or ill-considered legislation, but with no loss in terms of effective governability or stability. Similar provisions are well tried and tested in several other European nations, and there is no reason why they should not be beneficial in an independent Scotland.

If, however, it is felt that this proposed minority-veto referendum mechanism is too novel and radical, then some alternative provision for restraining the power of wayward governing majorities should be made. If we mean to enjoy balanced liberty rather than populism, a single chamber Parliament with unlimited legislative power is simply not a viable option. There are two possible choices. Either we could establish a strong second chamber, which is elected at different times, and in a different manner, from the first, and which is armed with the power to veto non-money bills unless over-ridden by a super-majority; or else, we could establish a strong directly-elected President with effective powers of veto (as in Portugal), or with the power to call a referendum on his or her personal initiative (as in Iceland). However, neither a second chamber nor a strong presidency would fit well with Scottish traditions. Both bring other problems greater than those they are intended to solve: a workable second chamber is difficult to construct in a unitary State[39], while a strong President (as well as being symbolically unacceptable to monarchists) could become a party-political leader and challenge the Prime Minister's executive authority. Therefore, while it might seem novel, a unicameral Parliament, in which majority-power is restrained by a minority-veto referendum mechanism, is actually the safest and most practical model for an independent Scotland.

Bills that have been passed by Parliament (or have been referred to and passed by the people) shall become laws on receiving royal assent. In the UK, as might be expected, the theoretical power to refuse assent has never been formally curtailed, but it has practically fallen into disuse by convention. Although some may argue that the Queen could, theoretically, in extreme and unspecified circumstances, refuse assent, it is reasonable to predict that she is unlikely to do so; any refusal of assent, even if for the best of motives, would surely precipitate a profound 'constitutional crisis'.

In Ireland, in contrast, the President, after consulting the advisory Council of State, may at his or her discretion refer a bill to the Supreme Court for advice on its constitutionality; the Supreme Court then decides on the constitutionality of the bill, and the President grants or withholds assent accordingly. The power to withhold assent has been transformed, in Ireland, from a perfunctory dead letter into a real, if occasional and extraordinary, check on the majority's tendency to legislative absolutism.

The Model Constitution follows the Irish example, except that the discretionary power is transferred from the Head of State (who in Scotland's case would be a hereditary monarch) to the Presiding Officer, whose duty it would be to refer any legislation of dubious constitutionality to the Supreme Court for advice. If the Supreme Court then rules that the bill is constitutional, the Presiding Officer would formally advise the Head of State to sign the bill, and promulgate it as law, without further delay. If the Supreme Court advises that the bill is in whole or part unconstitutional, the Presiding Officer would have to advise the Head of State to withhold assent and to return the bill to Parliament. Reference of bills to the Supreme Court in this manner is a form of *abstract* judicial review; it allows a bill to be tested for its constitutionality *before* it comes into force and *before* it damages the lives of citizens or the moral or institutional fabric of democracy.

It should be noted that this procedure complements, but does not replace, *concrete* judicial review. The Presiding Officer might decide not to refer a bill. The full consequences of a bill might not initially be apparent. Therefore, the fact that a bill was not referred to the Supreme Court by the Presiding Officer (and it is, after all, expected that this power will be used only sparingly), or the fact that the Court foresaw no constitutional objections, does not prevent a resulting law from being subject to concrete review should a case arise. It should further be noted that referral of a bill to the Supreme Court concerns only its constitutional validity, and not its merit or wisdom: the minority-veto / referendum procedure sees to that.

All democracies allow some delegation of legislative power from the Parliament to the executive. The power to make regulations, or 'secondary legislation', having the force of law, is necessary feature of representative government in a large and complex society with a mixed social-market economy. Even the best and most empowered Parliament has neither the time, nor the expertise, nor the impartiality, to deal with all the technical aspects of government and administration. Much of this delegated power will be entrusted, in a decentralised democracy applying the principle of subsidiarity, to local Councils, or to vocational bodies, whose secondary legislation can be tailored to the needs and conditions of those most affected.[d] There nevertheless remains a substantial a sphere of public life in which, for the sake of the common good, properly falls under the regulative activity of the Government, and which is most effectively handled by Ministers, advised and assisted by professional civil servants.

Yet this delegated power, which is quasi-legislative in nature, but is alienated from the legislature, is very dangerous. If not properly limited and circumscribed, it may pose a grave threat to liberty. A

---

[d] An example of this would be the delegation of the regulation and licensing of members of a profession to the vocational body representing that profession.

Government that can make law at will, and is not itself subject to laws agreed by the representatives of the community, is the very definition of absolutism. The question, then, is one of balance, moderation and proper constitutional safeguards. We must allow for the existence of delegated regulatory power, but place reasonable limits upon it to ensure that it serves the people and does not harm them. To this end, the Model Constitution allows legislative power to be delegated, subject, however, to the rule that all regulations or orders made under such delegation be laid before Parliament for at least 40 days before coming into effect. During this time, an appropriate select committee shall examine the regulation, and may, if there is any objection, bring it into the floor of Parliament for approval or rejection. Moreover, the permissible scope of delegation is restricted to 'specific purposes of a limited and technical nature' (a deliberately broad guideline, which will have to be clarified by experience). The delegation of legislative power in matters of taxation, personal rights, civil and criminal law, and the administration of justice, is prohibited.

A Parliament is not only a legislature but also a representative and deliberative chamber. The scrutiny and oversight of the executive branch are amongst its essential tasks. The Model Constitution therefore seeks to ensure that committees have adequate legal powers, the information and secretarial resources to support their work, and a stable and specialised (as opposed to fluid and generalist) membership. This means that the role and status of committees must be guaranteed by constitutional status. It is not acceptable to leave these matters to be regulated by the governing majority, since the Government would then be in a position to frustrate, or even undo, any beneficial reforms.

In particular, the Model Constitution provides for the election of parliamentary committees by proportional representation (rather than, say, appointment by the party whips, which enables committees to be used as a source of party patronage). In response to the common complaint that committees in the Scottish Parliament are too small, and that committee-members are as a result over-stretched and not able to concentrate fully on their duties, the Model Constitution fixes the minimum size of committees at 12 members; Ministers are excluded from membership of committees on the grounds of a conflict of interest.

The Model Constitution also allows for the appointment, by parliamentary resolution, of Boards of Enquiry and Royal Commissions. Boards of Enquiry are intended to look deeply into specific administrative problems, acts or failings – perhaps arising out of an unfavourable report from the Ombudsman, for example – and to conduct a quasi-judicial investigation from which the facts can be ascertained and lessons learned. Royal Commissions would generally have a more forward-looking brief, being established to examine and report on options for the development of new policies. Royal Commission and Boards of Enquiry may include members from outside parliamentary, chosen for their specialist knowledge or experience.

## Council of Ministers

The executive authority remains at the core of all government. It sets the direction of public policy, directs the administration, represents the State in external affairs and commands the armed forces. Indeed, without an executive, there is no government: a State under the rule of a despot, with neither a legislative assembly nor an independent judiciary to constrain him, might easily be imagined, but a State without an executive to actually *govern* – that is, to *rule* – it, would almost be a contradiction in terms. In all commonwealths, is in the executive branch that the forces of the community are concentrated and are directed to common purposes; other institutions exist primarily to support, constrain, advise, censure, direct, choose, scrutinise and legitimate the holders of executive power.

In common with most other European democracies, the Model Constitution would retain the parliamentary form of government. This means that the executive is headed by a Prime Minister, who is chosen by and responsible to Parliament. The Prime Minister presides over the Council of Ministers, which is dependent upon the confidence of Parliament for its continuance in office. Parliament, in relation to the executive, will have four principal functions: (i) to choose the executive; (ii) to discuss, adopt, amend, or reject, legislation, financial estimates and treaties, most of which will be proposed and introduced by the executive; (iii) to debate and consider matters of public concern, and thereby to keep the executive informed of the grievances and desires of the people; and (iv) to scrutinise the executive, to hold it to account, and ultimately to dismiss it from office.

There will therefore be a close and reciprocal relationship between the legislative and executive branches. Most Ministers will be drawn from amongst the leaders of the largest party or coalition of parties in the Parliament, and, except during periods of minority government, the Government will generally be able to enjoy the support of a majority of the members of Parliament. The parliamentary general election will remain the central moment of political life, since it will determine both the shape and composition of the Government and direction of its legislative agenda.

It is technically incorrect to say that a parliamentary government involves a fusion of the executive and legislative powers, as if these were concentrated in the same hands. On the contrary, in a well-functioning parliamentary system, the executive and legislature are clearly separated: the executive branch is unable to legislate, except through the legislature (Parliament), and the legislature is unable to administer or execute the law, except through the executive (Government). There is, however, a *mutual* subordination of these two powers. In ordinary circumstances, the legislature generally defers to the leadership of the executive. This does not mean that the legislature should act as a mere rubber stamp, blindly accepting everything that the executive proposes without amendment or reservation, but it does mean that the legislature expects the executive to play a major role in policy leadership and co-ordination, and is content – again, in normal circumstances – to confine itself to the role of scrutinising, amending, and adopting (or not) the proposals put to it by the executive. In extraordinary circumstances, nonetheless, the executive is revealed to be subordinate to the legislature. If the legislature is not content with the direction of leadership provided by the executive, or with its handling of the administration, then the legislature is empowered to dismiss the executive from office and choose another executive in its stead.[40]

In Britain, parliamentary government was most fully developed in the period between the first (1832) and second (1867) Reform Acts. It was during this period that the traditional liberal understanding of British parliamentary government was developed by Walter Bagehot. Bagehot's mistitled treatise, 'The English Constitution', described a system in which the Government and the House of Commons really did exist in a balanced relationship of mutual subordination. Bagehot's work depicted a powerful executive, which possessed both initiative and responsibility, but which could hold and exercise such power only in so far as it was able to carry before it the suffrages of a free and autonomous House of Commons. The House of Commons was able to act, in Bagehot's words, as an 'electoral college' in constant session: it could freely determine who would be Prime Minister (the legal choice, of course, was in the hands of the Monarch, but the temper and inclination of the House of Commons was decisive).[41] Moreover, the Commons had the power to enforce political responsibility; it could, and quite often did, remove wayward Prime Ministers from office. At a time when the maximum term of office of the House of Commons was fixed by law at seven years, the average tenure of a Prime Minister was about three and a half years; in between times, many Governments fell, or were forced to resign, as a result of losing the confidence of the Commons.

The trend over the last hundred and fifty years, since the extension of the franchise to the working class and the formation of mass parties, has been towards ever-increasing Prime Ministerial dominance. Despite attempts to hide behind its gothic architecture, arcane traditions and 'mother-of-Parliaments' rhetoric, the role of the Westminster Parliament as an independent legislature, and as an effective check on the power of the Government, has been steadily eroded. Westminster has become a place of theatrical, ritualised confrontation between the Government and Opposition, where laws are hurriedly enacted by well-whipped majorities without proper debate or scrutiny. As a democratic legislature and as a deliberative body it can only be regarded as dysfunctional.

The devolved Scottish Parliament was designed with this growing sense of general dissatisfaction against the workings of the Westminster Parliament in mind. From its conception, the Scottish Parliament was intended to offer a different type of democracy. It was intended to be more representative, more consensual and consultative, and less needlessly confrontational.[42] Most of all, it was intended to designed to deliver a truly parliamentary, rather than Prime Ministerial, democracy. Some of the steps taken to achieve this have been discussed in the preceding chapters, including proportional representation, fixed-term Parliaments, the stronger committee system, and increased parliamentary control over its own organisation and proceedings. One reform, however, which has not yet received as much attention as it deserves, is the rationalisation of relations between the Government and Parliament. It is to this reform, the importance of which cannot be underestimated, to which we now turn.

As a matter of strict law, the monarch of the United Kingdom can appoint anyone she pleases as Prime Minister. In fact, as a matter of strict law, the office of Prime Minister has no clearly-defined terms of reference. The office, with the myriad of powers and privileges surrounding it, has emerged from custom, convention and tradition. It is only convention that states that the Prime Minister must 'command a majority' in the House of Commons. It is only by convention that the Prime Minister must resign if he or she loses that majority. Thus no one has ever been elected as Prime Minister of the United Kingdom. Prime Ministers are simply appointed by the monarch, usually after a general election or an internal party transfer of power, without so much as a parliamentary vote to legitimise them (although it could be argued that the vote on the Queen's Speech acts, by convention, as an informal and belated 'vote of investiture'). Once appointed, the Prime Minister continues to hold office based on the implied consent of the House of Commons. If the Prime Minister loses such consent, for example by being defeated in the House on a government bill, he or she is generally expected – again, by custom and convention – to resign, or else to dissolve Parliament.[e]

The Scotland Act rejected these conventional relationships in favour of a legally binding mechanism of election and accountability. The First Minister is elected by the Scottish Parliament after each parliamentary election, and holds office until soon after the next parliamentary election, unless prematurely removed by a formal vote of no-confidence. This mechanism of election and responsibility is clear, direct and pleasingly democratic, as it gives the First Minister an unambiguous parliamentary mandate to govern. The symbolic contrast between the two systems is also very clear: in the British State, power comes from the Crown; in Scotland, it comes from the people.

One could, of course, argue that Westminster conventions work well enough, at least in a two-party system with artificially large majorities. As long as one party has an overall majority, and that party has a clearly designated leader, it is obvious who is to be Prime Minister. However, to rely on such conventional understandings in a multi-party Parliament, elected by proportional representation, in which multiple coalition arrangements are possible, would produce uncertainty. It could be unclear who has a mandate to govern. At least, it could place too much discretionary power in the Head of State, who might be able to influence the composition of the Government and so tilt the direction of policy. The election of the Prime Minister by Parliament removes both uncertainty and discretionary power; it places responsibility for forming a Government unequivocally in the hands of the parliamentary parties, and ensures that the resulting Government has an unambiguous parliamentary mandate.

Replacing the Westminster notion of informal tacit consent with a formal process of election and responsibility has the further

---

[e] The Fixed Terms Parliament Act of 2011 provides indirect statutory acknowledgement of some of these conventions, while clarifications of the conventions surrounding the appointment and dismissal of Governments are given in the Cabinet Manual – even so, these conventions are not legally enforceable and can lack certainty in their application.

advantage of allowing the Scottish Parliament to reject bills and amendments proposed by the Scottish Government, without thereby without calling the stability of the executive into question. As the life of the Scottish Government is not at stake on every vote, there is less need for whipping and for rigid party discipline.[f] Freed from the danger of being unseated by adverse votes, the Scottish Government, even when in a minority situation, may safely adopt a 'give-and-take' relationship with Parliament, and may accept defeats on particular bills or votes while confident in the knowledge that it will not necess- arily be thrown out of office. This strengthens the Scottish Parliament as a legislative body. Rather than having to accept everything the Scottish Government does on an 'all-or-nothing' basis, the Scottish Parliament – or the parties within it – have the potential to exercise some autonomous control over both legislation and public policy.

The Model Constitution, following the example of the Scotland Act, would therefore incorporate a similar system of rationalised relationships between the executive and the legislative branches. The Prime Minister would be elected by Parliament within 30 days after the first meeting of Parliament following a general election, or within 30 days after the death, resignation, or removal, of the former Prime Minister. The election would take the form of a binding nomination, made by a resolution of Parliament, in the same form and manner as are currently used by the devolved Scottish Parliament. If the Parliament fails to elect a Prime Minister within this specified time, then, and then only, does the Head of State, acting on the advice of the Presiding Officer, have the right to dissolve Parliament and call a new general election. It is to be hoped that this prospect will concentrate the minds of the party leaders, and encourage them to come to an agreement rather than risk the hazard, expense, and possible humiliation, of a new election so soon after the last one.

---

[f] Party discipline in the Scottish Parliament still tends to be quite strict – perhaps a little too strict. Nevertheless, particularly in cases where the governing party does not have an absolute majority, the effect is still to strengthen Parliament as a whole (although it is the party leaders, and not the individual MSPs, who have the main responsibility for policy-bargaining).

Once elected, the Prime Minister would continue in office until their successor is elected (or they are re-elected) – this election is, of course, to be held within 30 days of the first meeting of Parliament following the next general election. Being unable to pass a budget might be viewed as a resigning matter, but otherwise the Prime Minister would be immune from removal by a legislative defeat. Only a formal vote of no-confidence, clearly distinguished from any particular law or policy, would be competent to dislodge the Prime Minister from office.

The Prime Minister cannot, and should not, govern alone, but with the advice and assistance of colleagues – the Ministers responsible for the several executive departments. The Model Constitution therefore vests no executive power in the Prime Minister alone; all powers are vested in the 'Council of Ministers', a collegial body, consisting of the Prime Minister and the Ministers, which constitutes the formal executive of Scotland. This requirement to share power with colleagues prevents any one person having sole and absolute authority in the State.

On the other hand, the appointment of ministerial colleagues rests solely with the Prime Minister, who also presides over the Council of Ministers and acts as its chief executive. Ministers hold office during the pleasure of the Prime Minister, and may be dismissed at will; but they are individually responsible for their official acts, and are subject to the requirements of parliamentary confidence.

The office of Prime Minister, as set out in the Model Constitution, therefore involves a delicate balance between the principles of collegiality and leadership. The Prime Minister is not a sole ruler, since without ministerial colleagues to share in his or her rule, and to advise and assist the Prime Minister, the government cannot be carried on. Yet the Prime Minister is not merely one-amongst-equals, as the ministerial colleagues, being chosen and dismissed by the Prime Minister, are ultimately subordinate to him or her. The term 'premiership' is therefore fitting, as it implies precedence amongst a group of paradoxically 'subordinate equals'. The Prime Minister is 'first servant' of the people, yet shares this honour with ministerial colleagues, who, together with the Prime Minister, are ultimately responsible through Parliament to the people.

Hence Ministers have a heavy responsibility. Their duty is to give honest advice and assistance to the Prime Minister, and to support the Prime Minister in the realisation of the collective aims of the Government. Yet they must also check and restrain the Prime Minister, if need be, and must never allow themselves to become blind, passive instruments in the Prime Minister's hands. It is for this reason that Ministers are held individually responsible, both in law and before Parliament, for their actions. A Minister who disagrees with the Prime Minister on a matter of principle, and who, after private remonstration, can neither convince the Prime Minister to alter course, nor be reconciled in good conscience to the Prime Minister's plans, must resign from office.[43]

The actual balance of power between the Prime Minister and his or her fellow-Ministers will depend upon many things, not least the personal charisma, ability and leadership style of the Prime Minister. These circumstantial factors cannot be provided for in a Constitution. However, it is evident that, no matter how autocratic a Prime Minister would like to be, the constraints of coalition government enforce a more collegial style:

> The leaders of coalition governments are very differently placed. To begin with, they are bound by coalition pacts and understandings. They have not the power of appointment, allocation to departments, or dismissal in the case of those posts allocated to parties other than their own. Even if they want to, they cannot exert the kind of forceful leadership and management open to the leader of a single-party government. If necessary, they have to be prepared to tolerate public expression of disagreement with government policy by cabinet colleagues, and they are more likely to have to use cabinet committees, direct negotiations with the leaders of other coalition parties or similar devices to resolve policy differences.[44]

Therefore, to the extent that the Model Constitution encourages coalition Government, due to proportional representation, it can also be expected to promote a more collegial style of decision-making; although, as the 2011 election showed, proportional representation alone provides no guarantee.

The Model Constitution would limit the Prime Minister's powers of patronage and appointment in several significant ways. Judges are appointed by an independent Judicial Appointments Council, explained more fully in the next section. An independent Public Service Commission is intended to ensure the independence and political impartiality of the civil service, preventing the development of a 'spoils system' in which public offices are corruptly given in return for political favours. In contrast to the situation prevailing south of the border, Scotland has no established Episcopal church to which the Prime Minister might appoint bishops. Neither, in the absence of a Scottish House of Lords, would there be scope for patronage appointments to that body. There would be no grace-and-favour mansions to award, no ceremonial sinecures to distribute. In short, the whole form of government would be purged and rationalised, and the plethora of small but potent patronage powers available to a British Prime Minister would have no Scottish counterpart. These changes, each minor in itself, would have the cumulative effect of promoting a more balanced and moderated form of government, preventing the autocratic abuse of power, without undermining the stability or effectiveness of the executive.

In the same vein, the Model Constitution restricts the maximum number of persons who may simultaneously hold ministerial office to one-fifth of the total membership of Parliament. This provision, which is taken from MacCormick's draft, has two principal advantages. Firstly, it keeps the political executive to a manageable size: Ministers can have direct and personal access to the Prime Minister, the Government can act as effective collective body, and policies and priorities can easily be co-ordinated between departments. Secondly, limiting the number of Ministers will reduce the influence of payroll vote (the number of members of Parliament who, by holding ministerial office, are bound to support the Government line), thus increasing Parliament's independence from the Government.[45]

A further reform is to enable up to one-third of the Ministers to be appointed from outside Parliament. It is usual, in most parliamentary democracies, for Ministers to be recruited from amongst the members of Parliament. Situations might arise, however, in which it is beneficial to make certain ministerial appointments from outside of Parliament. This might reflect the need to appoint persons with particular experience and expertise to fulfil special ministerial functions. It might stem from a desire to allow certain ministers to concentrate on executive functions without the burden of constituency duties. It might even be a consequence of the lack of eligible candidates of ministerial calibre amongst the Government's parliamentary caucus. The usual expedient, in the Westminster system, is to appoint an externally recruited Minister to the House of Lords – it is a strong convention that Ministers must be members of one House or the other, in order to be able to speak up for their department and to answer parliamentary questions. Thus, when Alan Sugar became a Minister responsible for enterprise, despite having no parliamentary background, he was elevated to the House of Lords. Likewise, Admiral West was given a seat in the Lords upon his appointment as Minister for Security and Counter-terrorism. In an independent Scotland, without a House of Lords, some other expedient would have to be found. The easiest, best and most elegant solution would be to allow such extra-parliamentary Ministers to sit and speak (but not vote) in Parliament. There they would be able to answer questions, contribute to debates, and be properly held to account.

An independent Scotland, taking its place amongst the nations of Europe and the world, would determine its own foreign and defence policy. Scotland would have the authority to enter into treaties and agreements with other States, and, ultimately, to defend itself, or its legitimate interests, by force of arms, according to the norms of international law. The powers of war and peace, of alliance and compact, are necessary, then, for the defence, security and prosperity of Scotland; but these are also perilous powers, which can ruin the State if used recklessly, or if abused to serve the private interests of a few. It is therefore essential that these powers should be established, regulated and limited by the Constitution, and their use subordinated to the public good.

Here, as in other aspects of constitutional design, old Westminster habits, and the laws and customs of the British State, can teach us only what to avoid. Control of the armed forces and foreign relations, in the British State, are largely prerogative powers of the Crown. Parliamentary control is minimal; parliamentary supervision severely limited. Wars may be declared, and treaties ratified, by the sole decision of the Prime Minister, without so much as a parliamentary vote (although treaties do not become integrated into domestic law unless they are incorporated by enabling legislation). The concentration of such 'imperial' powers in so few hands, with so little restraint or accountability, has damaging effects: during the last ten years, Scottish soldiers have been killed and wounded in Afghanistan and Iraq, for no tangible public benefit, in spite of the anti-war stance of most of the Scottish people.

The Model Constitution, in common with the MacCormick draft and most modern democratic Constitutions, therefore requires that Parliament exercise control over war-making and treaty-making power. There are two points worthy of notice here. Firstly, Parliament's authority is required not only for formal declarations of war, but also for *any* deployment of armed forces on active service outside of Scotland. Such decisions require approval by a two-thirds majority vote, giving the opposition a veto-power. This rule would not apply, however, in situations where Scotland is facing actual, or imminent, enemy attack. Secondly, a two-thirds majority would also be required for the ratification of treaties which delegate powers to international organisations such as the European Union, in light of their quasi-constitutional character and their profound affect on domestic law.

## Judiciary

Every step away from absolutism and towards constitutional rule necessarily involves an increase in judicial power; for, if we prescribe legal and constitutional limits against arbitrary power, then we must create some sort of judicial body to decide when the rulers have exceeded those limits.

Nevertheless, this progress towards constitutional rule raises the deceptively simple, but false, argument that 'unelected judges' should not have the power to overturn the laws made by 'elected politicians'. It is easy to write an opinion-piece decrying the power of 'white, male, upper-class, out of touch judges' (or 'liberal-lefty activist judges', if you are on the other side). It is much harder to convey the importance of judicial review in the protection of liberty. It is therefore necessary to address this flawed argument head-on, and to show why judicial review of the constitutional validity of Acts of Parliament is a thoroughly democratic practice. This can be expressed in a series of axioms:

(i) That the people, in a constitutional liberal-democracy, ought to possess the sovereign power – that is, ultimately, the power to adopt and amend the Constitution;

(ii) That Parliament is *not* the people, merely a select body, usually of professional partisan politicians, which at best rather imperfectly represents the people;

(iii) That the powers of Parliament are not original, inherent or unlimited; they are merely delegated by the people under the terms of the Constitution, which is the supreme expression of the 'settled will' of the people;

(iv) That the Parliament must not violate the terms, or exceed the bounds, of its delegated authority;

(v) That there must be an independent judicial body with the right to decide whether any particular law is, or is not, consistent with the exercise of Parliament's delegated constitutional authority;

(vi) That a Supreme Court, in annulling an unconstitutional Act of Parliament, is therefore defending, and not frustrating, the will of the people; it is simply placing the higher and more fundamental law enacted by the people (i.e. the Constitution) above the lower law enacted by their representatives in a hierarchy of judicial norms.

Although strong judicial review may be alien to the British system of government and traditional Westminster-style notions of parliamentary sovereignty, it is not so alien to Scotland. The Scottish constitutional tradition has never fully accepted the English idea of the sovereignty of Parliament;[46] Scotland has maintained, despite pressure to conform to the expectations of the Westminster system, some belief in the democratic concept of sovereignty being vested in the people. In the famous words of the Declaration of Arbroath, we trust not in Kings or Parliaments, but in 'the whole community of the realm'.[47]

In the present devolved system, moreover, we already have a form of judicial review, in that the Scottish Parliament is not a sovereign body; the courts may declare acts of the Scottish Parliament invalid, and thus they protect the rights of the sovereign – Westminster. To say that the Scottish Parliament should become a 'fully sovereign body' is a mistake, for such a course of action would only replicate in Holyrood many of the flaws of Westminster. The solution is not to transfer sovereignty not from one Parliament to the other, but to transfer it from the British 'Crown-in-Parliament' to the people of Scotland. This not only means that the powers of the Scottish Parliament would be increased to encompass the whole range of what are now 'reserved matters', but that the Parliament itself should not be a sovereign body, and its laws should still be subject to judicial review in order to protect the sovereign people, from whom its powers are derived.[g]

The Model Constitution therefore provides for the establishment of a new body, a Scottish Supreme Court. This would sit above the Court of Session and the High Court of Justiciary, and would replace the Supreme Court of the United Kingdom.[h] The Scottish Supreme Court would hear, on appeal, all cases concerning the interpretation of the Constitution, or the constitutional validity of a law or treaty. It would also, as noted above, possess a limited *abstract* review

---

[g] There are certain parallels here with the operation of the Barrier Act in the Church of Scotland – the General Assembly is empowered to act, but it cannot act in certain areas without referring back to the Presbyteries.

[h] The UK Supreme Court is not a Supreme Court in the sense usually understood by constitutionalists, since, in the absence of a written and supreme Constitution, it has no power to annul Acts of Parliament on the grounds of their unconstitutionality. It does, however, act as a quasi-supreme Court with relation to Acts of the Scottish Parliament.

function, advising the Head of State or the Lord High Commissioner, when called upon to do so by the Presiding Officer, on the matter of whether or not to grant assent to laws.

Those who complain about the unrepresentative and unaccountable nature of the bench make a valid point. The answer, however, is not to deny constitutional jurisdiction to the courts, but to open up the judiciary, and to make judicial appointments more transparent, independent and meritorious. To this end, the Model Constitution creates a Judicial Appointments Council to nominate and appoint members of the judiciary.

The Judicial Appointments Council would consist of the Minister of Justice, as ex-officio convenor, the Lord Advocate as deputy convenor, two Senators of the College of Justice elected by their peers, one person elected by the Faculty of Advocates, and five lay representatives of the public (not being members of the judiciary or of the legal profession) to be elected by Parliament, by proportional representation and secret ballot, for four-year terms. This balanced arrangement would provide effective public scrutiny of judicial appointments, sufficient to ensure the quality, impartiality and representativeness of the bench, without enabling the Government, or the parties, or the existing judges, to solely dominate proceedings.

The Model Constitution also seeks to ensure the independence of judges once they have been appointed. They are declared to be subject only to the Constitution and the law, are forbidden from holding other offices, and are protected against arbitrary dismissal: judges may be removed only on the grounds of misconduct, negligence, or incapacity, by a two-thirds majority vote of Parliament. These rules, combined with secure salaries that cannot be reduced during their continuance in office, should render the judicial branch immune from partisan pressures and special interests.

## Local Government

Centralisation of power is, in essence, the negation of democracy. As power is centralised, it is necessarily concentrated into fewer and fewer hands. These hands, and the heads which direct them, are further away; they are, therefore, not only less intimately acquainted with the needs and aspirations of the people they are supposed to serve, but also more difficult to hold to account. Centralised authorities, as an inevitable consequence of their centralisation, are more rigid, more bureaucratic and more hierarchical in their structure; they are unreachable and remote, not only in terms of geographical location, but also in terms of 'social distance' and procedure.

There is a technological trend (perhaps even an inevitable, or nearly inevitable, trend) towards larger units. If these forces are to be liberating and not overpowering, they must be balanced by a renewed commitment to local democratic control. The local community, enjoying autonomy over many of the most important aspects of our daily lives, ensures that the individual is not left powerless in the face of distant and impersonal forces, but is able to exercise some autonomy within a smaller community of fellow citizens, which finds expression through local self-government.

Local government serves two functions. The first function is simply the provision of local services. These typically range from basic services like street cleaning and lighting, sanitation and refuse collection, through education, policing and health care, to the 'niceties of civilisation', such as libraries, theatres and museums. The second function of local government is to promote the community more widely, to act as an instrument of civic and economic renewal, and to contribute to a healthy democratic society. The importance of this civic, educative, democratising dimension to the well-being of the commonwealth ought never to be overlooked. We can have our own Parliament and Government, regular and free elections, a written Constitution and a Supreme Court, but without local autonomy our democracy would, most likely, remain fragile, shallow and apathetic.

To strengthen democracy, the civic spirit – the spirit of cooperation, participation and responsibility for the common good – must be inculcated and sustained. One of the best ways to achieve this to divide the country into substantially autonomous mini-polities, where politics can take place on a human scale, and in which citizens can learn the arts of self-government. These mini-polities, each with its own identity, political life, fiscal resources, priorities and concerns, and each under its own local democratic leadership, would not merely provide public services. They would also be sites of civic education and popular participation, empowering people and helping communities to articulate their own needs and priorities. They would teach us to relate to public authorities not as passive, individualistic consumers but as mutually responsible citizens.

Stronger local democracy would also permit a wider range of people to participate in self-government – not just as voters, but also as elected representatives and officials.[48] This promotes a broader, more inclusive political class, in which power is dispersed rather than being hoarded at the centre. It enables local 'aldermanic' elites (i.e. local small business owners, professionals and engaged citizens – the sort of people who attend the Rotary Club and the Guild, and who hold the civic life of a community together) to exercise effective and responsible leadership in their localities.

Autonomous mini-polities also encourage local spirit and local pride. They engender a healthy spirit of competition between the aldermanic elites of different communities, which is expressed through endeavouring to make their town or community 'better', in some visible and tangible way, than others. This competition has often has an aesthetic dimension. Centralisation builds things to a set plan. Buildings are commissioned by those who never have to live amongst them, and who never have to take any pride in them. Bureaucratic socialism builds concrete boxes, strictly utilitarian and devoid of beauty or spirit. Corporate capitalism also builds concrete boxes, but with ample parking and 24 hour automated check-outs. Mini-polities, on the other hand, have something of the renaissance city-state about them. In Victorian times, municipalities expressed their civic pride though the creation of beautiful parks, gardens and public buildings, from city halls and opera houses to public toilets. They patronised a vibrant civic architecture that infused public spaces with beauty, grace and personality. Restoring authority and autonomy to local government will not only redevelop the physical Scotland, scarred by the consequences of reckless industrialisation and catastrophic de-industrialisation; it will also, in subtle but certain ways, help to redevelop Scotland's people, scarred by years of despair, apathy and powerlessness.

Finally, the mini-polities would act as barriers to usurpation, or as nodes of lawful resistance against the arrogance of power. In this dense network of interlocking democratic institutions, intermediate bodies such as local councils are interposed between the individual and the State, preventing the former from being isolated and the latter from becoming absolutist. Thus they extend the life of democracy, as well as improving its quality. As Thomas Jefferson said:

> The republican government of France was lost without a struggle, because the party of *'un et indivisible'* had prevailed; no provincial organisations existed to which the people might rally under the authority of the laws.[i]

Regrettably, the tendency of Whitehall and Westminster since the Second World War has consistently been to overlook the civic, educative and democratic functions of local government, and to concentrate solely on the delivery of services at the minimum cost. Adopting this overly narrow concept of efficiency, it might seem absurd (especially from the perspective of a mandarin in Whitehall with limited knowledge of what lies north of Oxford) for Scotland – with a population smaller than Greater London – to be divided into dozens of ancient counties and burghs. The advantages of such 'inefficient' duplication and diversity, in terms of autonomy, civic pride, democratic engagement, responsibility and belonging were unseen or unacknowledged. Thus the Westminster Parliament passed the Local Government (Scotland) Act 1973, which, with little regard for historical boundaries or local feeling, centralised the provision of public services into nine great regions and about 50 districts. Old

---

[i] In order words, the Republic fell easily to Napoleon's coup, because the doctrine of Jacobin centralisation had prevailed, so there were no autonomous provincial bodies with the authority to organise lawful resistance to the coup in the name of the Constitution.

counties disappeared from the official map. Once-proud burghs were reduced to the status of mere 'communities'. Self-sufficient Burgh Councils, with their Provosts, staff and local rates, were abolished, to be replaced by so-called 'Community Councils', devoid of powers, purpose, finances and personnel. Another reform in 1996 abolished the regions (except for a few specialised regional services, such as policing) and created the current system of 32 unitary authorities, but did nothing to restore the autonomy of the burghs.

In the true sense of the word, then, Scotland today lacks any *local* government. Scotland's Councils cover only provincial, and not municipal, areas. They are broadly equivalent to English counties, German *Kreise*, French *Departements*, or Spanish *Provincias*. There is no real equivalent to the English town (civil parish), French *commune*, Spanish *ajuntamento*, or German *Gemeinde*.

This lack of small-scale local government costs Scotland dearly, especially outside of the four big cities. It means that there is no-one responsible for the overall well-being of places such as Motherwell or Airdrie. No one cares, solely and entirely, for the redevelopment of Paisley or Ayr. Nobody's honour, fame or political career rests on restoring Tain's prosperity, or cleaning up Inverkeithing, or getting Biggar back to work. All these tasks have been 'efficiently' centralised. Responsibility has been shifted to other people: to overstretched and anonymous administrators in remote Council chambers 50 miles away; to government officials in Leith or Whitehall; to people who, for whatever reason, lack the resources, presence, knowledge, inspiration, initiative and incentive to do very much about it. In Scottish town after Scottish town, the 30-year absence of a visible, authoritative and responsible civic leadership at the burgh level is evident in a depressing spiral of descent into despair and disrepair.

The Model Constitution sets out to change this slide into centralised control. It would inject a revitalising double dose of decentralisation into Scotland's body-politic. Firstly, Scotland would be divided into an 'upper tier' of Districts and Cities, which would be based, at least initially, on the existing boundaries of the 32 unitary authorities. Each District and City would be governed by an elected

Council, chosen by proportional representation in the manner prescribed by law. Parliament would be able to devolve a wide range of legislative, executive and fiscal powers to these Councils, covering policy areas such as health, education, culture, the arts, transport, infrastructure, planning, housing, economic development and environmental protection. Secondly, the Model Constitution would enable Districts and Cities, within a general framework established by law, to be sub-divided into a number of 'lower tier' authorities, consisting of the restored Burgh Councils and reinvigorated Community Councils, with proper budgets and paid staff, to which certain powers could be delegated.

This system of flexible double-devolution is made necessary by the diversity of Scotland. Although a relatively small country,[j] Scotland is far from homogenous: it might only be about 40 miles along the M8 from Edinburgh's New Town to Glasgow's East End, but socially, culturally and economically they are worlds apart. Moreover, Scotland has no one metropolitan centre. Edinburgh is the capital, the seat of law, government and administration; but Glasgow holds the demographic and economic ascendency. Inverness and Aberdeen are the acknowledged regional capitals of the Highlands and of the North East respectively. This multi-polarity is advantageous – at once diversifying and unifying – since it prevents the stultifying concentration of influence, money and connections, in just one place. It means, however, that each part of the country, with its own historical and cultural identity, its own demographic composition, geography, and economic core, makes different demands on public policy. In matters such as education, policing, health, economic development and transportation one size cannot possibly fit all. The wide range of population densities exacerbates the problem, and calls for variably scaled solutions. Whether in terms of economic development, health,

---

[j] The emphasis here is on the word 'relatively'. Scotland, whether measured by area, population or resources, is by European standards a medium-sized country. It is only referred to as a small country because of its diminished status as a region of the UK.

education, public transport, environmental protection, or almost any other area of public life, the needs of Fort Augustus or North Berwick are not those of Glasgow or Aberdeen, while off-shore islands have their own set of priorities. Indeed, the needs of two towns in the same District – say Dunblane and Callander, or Kinross and Perth, or Ullapool and Thurso – can be remarkably distinct.

The operative principle is that of subsidiarity, which requires that all decisions should be taken at the most local level, except when it is necessary, in the common good, for decisions to be taken at a higher level. In the application of this principle, however, the Model Constitution, as befits a fundamental law dealing only with enduring principles, cannot be overly prescriptive. It therefore allows wide discretion to Parliament in seeking to balance local autonomy with the need for proper inspection and co-ordination, and for nation-wide minimum standards.

This is always a delicate balance. On the one hand, local auto-nomy means that different communities will chose to do different things, with different priorities, in different ways. Some places will be better run than others. Tabloids will raise 'postcode lottery'-type objections. So be it. This is authentic liberty, the freedom to be different, to show initiative, and to act without waiting for superior orders. The proper check on this liberty, in normal circumstances, is not the central Government, but the local people, through the ballot-box at local elections. On the other hand, autonomy does not mean a total lack of accountability – the common good must be maintained. The Model Constitution therefore subordinates local authorities to the jurisdiction of the Ombudsman and Auditor-General, who are to protect the people against maladministration and peculation, and to the ordinary courts, who are to protect fundamental rights, whilst also ensuring that local Councils do not exceed their devolved powers. Rules regarding freedom of information would also apply to local Councils.

This double decentralisation has the potential to revitalise our public life and to ensure the quality and diversity of Scotland's democracy, liberating local communities as the 'vital nuclei' of our regeneration.[49] Yet, if this intention is to be realised, local Councils

must be worthy of their enhanced powers. It is necessary to improve the effectiveness, visibility, and accountability, as well as the calibre and quality, of local Councils. One vital reform has already been achieved: the election of Councillors by proportional representation. This reform, which is enshrined in the Model Constitution, has already greatly diminished, if not yet fully eliminated, the number of 'One Party Regimes' in Scotland. Under the old electoral system, the mediocre party hacks, the faintly reeking products of corrupt urban machine politics, were often safely installed in office until removed by an earthquake or a party coup; now they find themselves accountable to the people and liable to be dislodged from power by dissatisfied voters.

Secondly, the decision-making process of District and City Councils must enable them to cope with the exercise of these more expansive powers. The Model Constitution offers two ways of achieving this. The standard way, which builds on existing practice, would be for Councils to continue operating under a quasi-parliamentary system. Under this system, the Council would be a representative, deliberative, scrutinising and legislative assembly. Its executive functions would be performed by a local 'cabinet' under the leadership of a 'Council Leader', chosen by and accountable to the Council according to the normal rules of parliamentary democracy. The Council Leader would hold a salaried office with certain statutory executive powers, while the functions of the Chief Executive Officer (a permanent and unaccountable official) might be correspondingly diminished. Although not mandated by the Model Constitution, provision might also be made for the establishment of 'Overview and Scrutiny' committees, composed of all Councillors not serving in executive positions, to help hold the executive to account. These committees might be chaired by the leader of the main opposition group on the Council. Potentially, these arrangements could lead to a more lively and responsible local election campaigns, in which the recognised leaders of the main party groups compete, on their record and their promises, as the local equivalents of 'Premier' and 'leader of the opposition'.

Alongside the Leader there would be a Lord Provost, Provost, or

Convenor,[k] who would occupy a civic and ceremonial position, and would combine chairing the Council with a representative function as the head of the District or City. As well as providing effective local leadership backed by a majority party or coalition in the Council, this system also has the benefit of providing a convenient division of labour: while the Council Leader delivers strategic policy for the City or District, the Lord Provost or Convenor is free to open fetes, greet dignitaries, and promote the cultural life of the community.

In addition to this local 'cabinet' system, the Model Constitution also provides for a more radical approach to empowering the decision-making structures of local government: the adoption of directly elected 'executive Provosts'. These civic leaders would combine executive powers with broader civic and representative functions. In this respect, Scotland may learn a salutary lesson from London. Whether loved or hated, both Ken Livingstone and Boris Johnson have been strong, popular Mayors, who have for the most part served London well, and have met the challenge of bearing both power and responsibility. Directly-elected Lord Provosts in our cities, with real powers and responsibilities, and clear public mandates, might be similarly capable of revitalising local democracy in Scotland. Like the Mayors of London, it is to be hoped that directly-elected executive Lord Provosts will achieve national recognition and become household names – their reputations will be made or broken on the strength of, say, Dundee's education system, or Aberdeen's new approach to public transport. The prospect of such national recognition (and the ability to make a real practical difference, given adequate powers and resources) would encourage stronger candidates to come forward.

## Ombudsman, Auditor-General and Independent Commissions

In a modern, party-based representative democracy, the responsibility of the Government to Parliament, and of Parliament to the

---

k These terms are effectively synonymous – the only difference, from the point of view of this Model Constitution, being that a Lord Provost presides over a City Council, while a Convenor or Provost presides over a District Council.

people, although essential, cannot be relied upon to prevent every possible abuse of power. As long as the Government is supported in Parliament by a loyal majority party or a by solid coalition, there is temptation to manipulate the system for partisan ends, or to suit the convenience of incumbents. To overcome this temptation, it is necessary to create additional external checks, which lie outside the parliamentary chain of delegation and accountability, and are insulated from party-politics.[50] These external checks may be regarded as 'integrity branch' institutions; they are not part of the legislative, executive or judicial powers, but sit outside this traditional structure, ensuring that the three active branches are able to perform their duties in accordance with basic principles of good governance, such as transparency, accountability, due process and fairness.[51]

The MacCormick draft does not mention these integrity-branch institutions, and would leave them, where they exist at all, to the mercy of parliamentary majorities. This would weaken their status and powers, and render them less able to stand up against a wayward Government. In contrast, the Model Constitution insists that integrity-branch institutions be given entrenched constitutional status, with guaranteed powers and genuine autonomy from the Government and the parliamentary majority.

Hence, in addition to the Judicial Appointments Council mentioned above, the Model Constitution makes provision for: (i) an Ombudsman, to protect the people against maladministration, and to provide a means of redress for grievances against public authorities; (ii) An Auditor-General, to keep watch over public finances and ensure that public monies are properly accounted for; (iii) an Electoral Commission, to supervise the holding of elections and referendums and to ensure they are freely and fairly conducted; (iv) a Public Service Commission, to ensure the integrity, impartiality, competence and professionalism of the civil service; (v) A Freedom of Information Commission, to enforce a culture of openness and transparency in government; and (vi) a Broadcasting Commission, to ensure a free media and to provide the impartial regulation of public broadcasting which is so essential to a representative democracy.

The Ombudsman and the Auditor-General are each to be appointed by Parliament, on a non-partisan basis, by a two-thirds majority vote. Their terms of office are fixed at six years, during which they shall enjoy a guaranteed salary; they may only be dismissed from office on the grounds of gross misconduct, neglect of duty or incapacity. While subject to the general rules laid down in the Constitution and by law, the Ombudsman and Auditor-General are to be independent of Parliament and the Government in the execution of their duties. They shall have the power to initiate their own investigations, as well as to receive petitions. They may inspect all official documents, may require redress of grievances, and may bring cases to court if legal action is required. Their jurisdiction is to include not only Ministers and civil servants, but also local government and other persons acting in the service of the State; this means that institutions such as the police, the armed forces, public corporations, and state-sponsored bodies, will not be able to avoid scrutiny. Finally, to assist them in these duties, the Model Constitution allows for the appointment of Deputies if required. These constitutional provisions (which, incidentally, would do little more than entrench the relevant provisions of the existing Public Services Ombudman (Scotland) Act 2002 and of Section 69 of the Scotland Act 1998) should provide the status, powers and autonomy needed for the Ombudsman and Auditor General to perform their duties.

The other integrity branch institutions, the Electoral Commission, Public Service Commission, Freedom of Information Commission and Broadcasting Commission, are constituted as boards of seven members. These, like the Judicial Appointments Council discussed previously, have a 'mixed' or 'balanced' membership, with members elected by Parliament to represent the public sitting alongside members who are chosen on a non-partisan basis in accordance with their qualifications and experience.[1]

---

[1] Serious consideration was given to the inclusion of randomly-selected members of the public, who would be chosen in a manner similar to juries, to serve a term as Participant Observers on these integrity-branch Commissions. Random lot is very a useful device for such institutions, where a-rationality independence from any special interest is of greater value than, say, being representative of a particular strand of opinion (see Dowlen, 2008).

## Fundamental Rights and Freedoms

Human rights and civil liberties in the UK have been under threat for several decades. The erosion of liberty began in earnest under Margaret Thatcher, who wanted strong coercive powers in order to deal with trade unions and economic unrest. It accelerated during the 1990s, as both Labour and the Conservatives became involved in a tabloid-fuelled bidding war to appear tough on crime. The World Trade Centre attack of 11 September 2001, and the resulting 'War on Terror', only exacerbated the situation. Now civil liberties that were once taken for granted, such as habeas corpus,[m] due process of law and trial by jury have been suspended in the fatal name of 'security'.

The most worrying aspect of this increase in State power is the rise of the 'Surveillance State'. The Government keeps a running check on our internet usage and our phone calls, and allows the data to be accessed, without our knowledge or consent, and often without a judicial warrant, by a wide range of public authorities, for all sorts of unexpected purposes.

Those who think they have 'nothing to hide' might be untroubled by this intrusion into their private lives, and might believe that the benefits, in terms of catching criminals and preventing terrorist attacks, outweigh the costs. Such a careless and cavalier approach to privacy, however, cannot be entertained by those who value liberty and who understand the workings of power: *liberty* requires privacy for citizens and transparency for the State, but *power* demands the opposite. A people who are tracked, monitored, inspected and overseen cannot be free. They cannot dissent. They cannot organise. The reason is quite simple – that everyone has something to hide. It might not necessarily be something illegal: it

---

[m] In the technical sense, 'habeas corpus' is an English writ and alien to Scots law. The Liberation Act of 1701 performed an equivalent function in Scotland, protecting people against 'wrongous imprisonment'. The term 'habeas corpus' is understood in this context as a general principle that no-one should be imprisoned without the due process of law.

might just be an affair, or a secret about one's sexuality, or a bit of gambling in the past, or perhaps a youthful flirtation with soft drugs. Besides, there are so many laws, most of which we are ignorant of and can practically ignore, that most of us probably do something illegal every day. It might be something as simple as discarding an apple core in an improper place, or being a bit late in catching up with the paperwork and forgetting to tell the DVLA that you have moved house. For most people, most of the time, it is not a problem. The press do not have the desire to expose, and the police do not have the resources to punish, most of these minor peccadillos.

But what if you are a 'dissident', a whistleblower, a campaigner for justice? Then it is different. Then the regime which uses such powers of surveillance can silence you by blackmail, or harass you into submission, or find some way to either ridicule or punish you. Before dismissing this as a paranoid dystopian fiction, we should pause to remember that powers of secret surveillance have always been at the root of organisations such as the Stasi and the KBG, and have been used to silence, repress and harass opposition in many countries – even ones that are not openly totalitarian.

The British State is not above this: it has been reliably claimed that the powers of the surveillance state have been routinely used against environmentalists and anti-globalisation protestors.[52] This informational imbalance between the State and people makes it difficult to dissent and costly to oppose. The consequences are fatal to the health of democracy: it strangles civic life, closes debate and forces people into silenced passivity.

If we wish to preserve democracy, the restoration of traditional civil liberties, and in particular the right to privacy, freedom of association and assembly, freedom of protest, freedom of speech, the due process of law, and habeas corpus must therefore be a priority.[53] To repeal the worst of illiberal legislation passed in recent decades, as proposed by the Liberal Democrats in their 'Freedom Bill', would be a good start. It is unlikely, however, that merely repealing the offending laws would, in the long term, be sufficient. Such are the pressures and temptations on a Government, that whatever good is done by a general repeal is likely to be reversed, in short order, by a future administration. Fundamental rights and liberties must be enshrined in the Constitution – a higher law, superior to ordinary legislation, which can be amended only with a broad parliamentary and popular consensus, and which is upheld by an independent judicial power.

One straightforward way to achieve this aim of entrenching rights would be to incorporate the European Convention on Human Rights into the Scottish Constitution. This arrangement would build on the current statutory mechanism, which requires that all laws passed by the Scottish Parliament be compatible with the European Convention. However, while this would surely be improvement on not having a bill of rights at all, the European Convention offers only limited protection against the arbitrary power of the State. It contains, for example, no protection for trial by jury.

The European Convention has also been criticised for guaranteeing rights in one breath and rescinding that guarantee with the next. In many instances, the rights that it offers can be subject to general and vaguely-worded restrictions, which give the State the ability to limit and curtail the exercise of those rights for all sorts of reasons, including such spurious-sounding grounds as the protection of 'public morality' or 'public health'. Yet, these restrictions and limitations are, in turn, limited and restricted: they may be adopted only for certain purposes, they must be reasonable and proportionate to these purposes, and acceptable in a democratic society. The principal effect of the European Convention is not, therefore, to put absolute limits on the power of the State, but to declare a principle that certain fundamental rights should always be respected, and to require the Government to justify and explain any restriction of these rights, against the criteria of what is reasonable in a democratic society.

This is, in part, because the European Convention was intended not as a comprehensive set of rights, but only as a backstop – an absolute baseline below which no civilised country ever ought to fall. It was meant to supplement and to reinforce, but never to replace, the more specific, and more expansive, fundamental rights provisions of national Constitutions. The Model Constitution, following the MacCormick draft, therefore takes the European Convention as its point of departure, but builds on it to make a more robust document. It includes certain additional rights where required, clarifies some of the rights which are only implied or doubtful, and limits the scope of allowable restrictions.

In addition to traditional civil liberties and legal-procedural rights included in the European Convention, the Model Constitution – again, in imitation of MacCormick's text – includes certain socio-economic rights. It is recognised that this is a divisive issue, which separates individualist liberals from those of a more communitarian (social democratic, Christian-democratic or civic-republican) persuasion. However, it seems reasonable and self-evident that, in any society, the distribution of power will reflect the distribution of wealth, and that the economic 'constitution' of a polity ought therefore to receive as much attention as its political Constitution.

In particular, it is clear that a society in which property is widely distributed amongst a great number of moderately prosperous families will be more democratic than a society in which property is concentrated, either in the hands of the State, or an oligarchy of the very rich, or large corporations. In historical terms, a society of land-owning peasants, self-employed artisans and tradesmen, and independent small merchants, can hardly fail to sustain a good and democratic government. A society, on the other hand, in which productive property is engrossed by banks and soulless corporations,[n] and

---

[n] The word 'soulless' is not just a rhetorical flourish, nor an aesthetic complaint against the sterility of design, lack of humanity and false cheer of most chain stores. It refers instead to the fact that corporations, being 'artificial persons' created by law, have no soul, no conscience, no pity and no sense of honour. The human persons in charge of corporations might, individually, be good people, but they are trapped inside a system of rules, conventions and incentives, based on a false understanding of human need, which steers them into making corporate decisions that, while good for the share price, can have terrible consequences for workers, customers, environment and the community at large.

which dooms the vast majority of the people to debt-bondage and wage-slavery, will be able to enjoy, even at best, only a shallow, superficial and short-lived democracy.

There are four reasons for this. Firstly, the excessive concentration of wealth gives well-funded interests an unfair advantage in political competition, as can be seen in the connection between campaign finance and special-interest politics in the USA and many other countries. Secondly, extremes of gross wealth and poverty provide a breeding-ground for jealousy, distrust, violence and extremism, which can polarise a polity and undermine its stability, its capacity for compromise, and its ability to even consider (let alone achieve) the common good of all citizens. Thirdly, the poor are politically marginalised. In general, they are poorly informed about politics and less likely to vote. If not marginalised, they can easily be manipulated by demagogues, machine-politicians and factious leaders. Fourthly, and perhaps most importantly of all, the coexistence of excessive wealth and poverty destroys the very spirit of democratic conviviality. In the absence of their own productive property, many people are forced to hire out their labour to the rich; this subjects them to the lordly power (*dominium*) of the rich, who, by their arbitrary power of hiring and firing, can decide whether a poor person should be allowed to flourish, or should be driven into poverty or even destitution. This breeds arrogance and ostentation in the rich, and forces the poor into a submissive posture. It divides society into 'orders' and 'classes', undermining our human dignity and hindering the development of democratic confidence and civic virtue.

The solution advocated by both civic republican and the Christian-democratic traditions was to structure the law of property in such a way as to prevent the excessive concentration of wealth. James Harrington, arguably the greatest English civic republican author of the Civil War era, proposed that no one should be able to inherit more than a certain maximum amount of land; the rest would be taken in the form of an inheritance tax and redistributed.[54] This plan for a so-called 'Agrarian Law' was intended not just to prevent the accumulation of excessive wealth by the rich, but also, and perhaps more fundamentally, to dissuade the rich from *wishing* to accumulate excessive wealth, and to convince them to turn their efforts and energies to public service rather than private gain. A more modest proposal, suggested by Thomas Jefferson in his 1776 draft Constitution, was to replace the law of primogeniture (by which estates passed entire to the eldest son) with the law of gavelkind (by which they were to be divided between all heirs).[55] This, he argued, would ensure the division and redistribution of great fortunes over just a few generations, and prevent the rise of an oligarchy – although, of course, he did not reckon on the rise of the corporation, a body that does not die.

It should be noted that neither Harrington nor Jefferson wished, as Marxists wish, to *abolish* property. Their goal was not *common ownership* but *the most widespread diffusion of private ownership*. This is a vital distinction. Moreover, they did not aim at complete equality. They hoped only to ensure that most citizens would be moderately prosperous, so that none would have to demean themselves in order to live, and so that none would be capable of lording over others. Citizens enjoying this measure of moderate prosperity were thought to be well suited to a democratic life: they could live on friendly terms with all, without having to bow or scrape.

It is doubtful whether a proposal for an 'Agrarian Law' would meet with much approval today. In marginal ways, through land reform and reform of the inheritance laws, planning law, corporate law, and the laws governing competition, monopolies and mergers, practical steps could be taken to promote the wider distribution of productive property – but that is probably about it, short of a more profound and revolutionary change.

Thus the socio-economic dimension to freedom cannot be ignored. What sort of democracy is it, if the rich are able to dominate public life, and the poor are marginalised and excluded? What sort of liberty is there, if many do not have the basic resources, security or dignity of life and condition necessary to be full members of society? Where is the 'common good', if 'the least of these my brethren' are marginalised, exploited or dehumanised? What sort of 'commonwealth' is it, if wealth is engrossed by a tiny minority, and if the ordinary people are left to shift for themselves?

However, there are both principled and pragmatic grounds for being sceptical of the constitutional provision of socio-economic rights, which must be addressed. The principled argument rests on the view that social and economic policies are inherently, and quite rightly, a matter of party-political controversy. Even if there is a broad commitment to the notion that 'there is such a thing as society', and that in a civilised society risks and rewards must to some extent be shared, we do not all agree about how to proceed or how far to go. The proper role of the State in the regulation and fostering of the community, and the ways and means by which the State, market, family, church and voluntary sector ought each to be involved in the realisation of our common good, must be worked out by the community itself, in every time and place, through the ordinary practice of democratic politics, and in humble recognition that opinions will necessarily differ. This is one of the reasons why we have different political parties, offering the people not only alternative teams of potential governors, but also different ideas about what the priorities, functions and limits of government should be. This difference of ideology and opinion makes the constitutionalisation of social and economic rights seem undemocratic, since their inclusion would tend to undermine normal democratic procedures by prescribing certain pre-decided policy outcomes.

The pragmatic objection to the inclusion of socio-economic rights in the Constitution is that these rights tend to create positive duties, which often require public spending and active commitment on the part of the State in order to realise them. This makes it very difficult for the Courts to enforce these rights. If one has a constitutional 'right' to healthcare, and such healthcare is not provided in an adequate and timely manner, is the proper response to sue the Government? Can the Courts compel the Government to spend more on healthcare? The danger is either that the judges cease to be neutral defenders of basic rights, and become arbiters of socio-economic policy, or else that the Constitution becomes a 'dead letter'.

The Model Constitution overcomes these problems by referring to socio-economic rights without making them directly justiciable. It places a clear moral and constitutional duty upon Parliament to enact laws providing for socio-economic rights. It declares that the State has a duty, in principle, to protect the weak, to provide public services, to regulate the market, and to promote the common good, but it leaves the political decisions of how to apply these principles, and how to translate them into enforceable rights, to the ordinary processes of parliamentary democracy. For example, in order to ensure desirable employment practices, the Model Constitution empowers Parliament to regulate conditions of work, hours, wages, days of rest, holidays, and like matters.° Likewise, the Model Constitution establishes the clear and undeniable responsibility of Parliament to provide for universal public healthcare, public education, pensions and social security, but leaves it up to Parliament to decide how best to achieve these ends. This approach charts a middle course between, on the one hand, a narrowly individualist Constitution which is blind to the socio-economic foundations of democracy, and, on the other, one which is so detailed as to bind the hands of Parliament, or so prescriptive as to turn judges into policy-makers.

## Miscellaneous Provisions

The penultimate Article, entitled 'Miscellaneous Provisions', requires little further comment. It deals largely with matters that are more symbolic than substantive, such as the status of the capital city, the national flag and anthem and oaths of office. It does, however, contain several matters of more substantial importance, which need to be briefly discussed.

---

° This is necessary in order to avoid decision like the infamous Lochner case. The Lochner case held that a New York statute limiting the work of bakers to 10 hours a day and 60 hours a week was an 'unreasonable, unnecessary and arbitrary interference with the right and liberty of the individual to contract' See: Lochner v. New York, 198 US 45 (1905) Under the Model Constitution, thanks to these principles, such a decision would not occur – the right of Parliament to regulate the market for the good of all is endorsed.

Firstly, it prescribes the basic norms of behaviour required of public servants, stating that they are expected to 'perform their duties solely for the public interest' and that their integrity should not be compromised by any private interest or gain. It requires the Public Service Commission to adopt a Code of Conduct for public servants and empowers Parliament to give legal force to that Code.

Secondly, for the avoidance of doubt, provision is made for the holding of optional, consultative referendums (in addition to the binding minority-veto referendums and referendums on constitutional changes). These consultative referendums may be called by Parliament or by local Councils on proposed legislation or on any matter of general policy within their respective areas of competency.

Thirdly, it establishes a Consultative Assembly, in which economic, social and cultural interests are represented. This, like the minority-veto referendum mechanism, is intended as a partial substitute for the role of a second chamber. The Consultative Assembly provides a means for the socio-economic interests of society to express themselves in a public forum. This forum is modelled on similar institutions in France, Belgium, the Netherlands and other European states. Its purpose is to bring together the organised groups so that they may deliberate and advise Parliament and the Government on policy and legislation. In contrast to Parliament, which represents people on the basis of their opinions, structured through political parties and geographic constituencies, the Consultative Assembly would represent people according to their callings, trades and occupations. It is not a legislative second chamber, as it has neither the power to pass, nor introduce, nor veto, legislation. It can nevertheless function in a way analogous to a second chamber; it acts as a place of review and discussion away from the strictures of party politics, for example, and it provides a means whereby 'ordinary people', who are not full-time party-politicians, may become directly involved in public life.

A Consultative Assembly is not essential so that each specific interest can better make its voice heard – for this they can do, as separate groups and communities, without having a common body in which they all participate. Rather, it is essential so that the various interests can learn to understand and appreciate *other* interests. Representatives of workers should sit with businessmen and professionals, artisans with the farmers, sceptical secular academics with clergy. In meeting together to discuss matters of social and economic concern, each diverse group will learn that its own perspective, while valid, is not the only one, and that its particular interests, while important, cannot necessarily take precedence over the interests of others. In representing diverse interests, the members of the Consultative Assembly become negotiators and co-ordinators, whose resolutions help to discover a common good. This is a practical application of the principle of consensus democracy, which aims not just to serve the interests of the majority, but, as far as possible, the common good of all.[56]

The Model Constitution enables the Prime Minister of Scotland to appoint Special Advisors. These 'spads' are chosen by and responsible to the Prime Minister, on a party-political basis, and have a strategic policy advice or co-ordination role freed from the constraints of professionalism and impartiality imposed on the civil service. The utility of such 'Spads' to the Prime Minister cannot be doubted. However, an over-reliance on them, to the detriment of Ministers who must appear in, and be responsible to, Parliament, poses a danger to democracy. For this reason, their number is limited to 12 (as it used to be, until recently). The Code of Conduct for public servants would regulate the rules of their behaviour and provide for a clear demarcation of roles between 'spads', civil servants and ministers.

Finally, the Model Constitution regulates States of Emergency. The Council of Ministers may declare a State of Emergency in times of war or other severe public emergency. The declaration of a State of Emergency would give the Council of Ministers the authority to issue decrees having the force of law. These decrees would be able to restrict or suspend some of the procedural rights and civil liberties of citizens, relating to trial by jury and freedom of assembly, association and movement. It is necessary, even in the best democratic Constitutions, for such a power to exist. Times of grave crisis or emergency call for the sudden exercise of an effective power which is sufficient to maintain order, to uphold the law, to co-ordinate the defence of the realm, and to ensure the functioning of essential utilities like water supplies, fire-fighting and ambulance services. The absence of such a power could mean the ruin of the *res publica* and the collapse of our dream of independence, freedom and justice. Yet, the abuse of such power would also bring about the same ruin and collapse. For this reason, the scope and duration of such powers must be carefully regulated. There must be a legal, legitimate and orderly way of proclaiming such powers, of exercising them and of laying them down again. The Model Constitution therefore requires that a State of Emergency shall not remain in force for more than seven days, after which it shall lapse, unless approved by a two-thirds majority vote of Parliament. Parliament may extend a State of Emergency for up to three months and may renew it at three-monthly intervals for as long as the emergency necessitating it continues. During the State of Emergency, the Council of Ministers would not have absolute power. All decrees issued under its emergency powers would be subject to scrutiny by a Review Committee consisting of the Presiding Officer, two judges of the Supreme Court, and 12 members of Parliament elected by their peers. This Review Committee would have the authority to veto decrees on the grounds that they are unconstitutional or unnecessarily burdensome or oppressive. These provisions should ensure that Scotland has an effective mechanism for concentrating the power of the state when necessary to save democracy, without inadvertently destroying that which it is trying to protect.

## Adoption and Amendment of the Constitution

A flexible Constitution, one which may be amended by the ordinary legislative process, is hardly worthy of the name, since it puts the rights of every citizen, and the powers and privileges of every balancing institution, at the mercy of the parliamentary majority – that is, generally speaking, at the mercy of the Government. The Model

Constitution, then, is of the rigid type, in that it may not be amended by ordinary legislative process.

However, excessive rigidity, if it deprives the State of the ability to change and adapt to new circumstances and emerging popular desires, is almost as much to be feared as excessive flexibility. A good Constitution should take the middle course: it should be protected against hasty or partisan amendment, but open to improvement, when such improvements have broad support, both across Parliament and amongst the public.

The Model Constitution relies on two complementary means of constitutional entrenchment. Firstly, an amendment must be proposed by a two-thirds majority vote of Parliament. This protects against narrow, hasty and partisan amendments – although, in itself, it offers no guarantee that the Government and Opposition will not conspire against the people. Secondly, proposed amendments must be approved by the people – by the whole community of the realm – in a compulsory and binding referendum. This is a necessary consequence of the principle of popular sovereignty.[P] The two mechanisms together should ensure that beneficial amendments, which can achieve an elite consensus and popular approval, can be made, whilst ensuring against the dangers of usurpation.

The Model Constitution introduces two further checks. Firstly, no amendment may be proposed during a State of Emergency, nor during the enemy occupation of the country. This rule is designed to ensure that catastrophic circumstances are not exploited as an excuse to overthrow liberty. Its absence cost the French Republic its life in 1939, when a rump of Deputies, fleeing from German guns, voted power into the hands of Petain. Secondly, the Model Constitution requires that the referendum on constitutional amendments be held at the same time as the next parliamentary general election.

---

[P] States in which the Constitution may be amended by two legislative decisions, with a general election in between, such a Belgium and Sweden, also adhere to the principle of popular sovereignty, in as much as an amendment cannot be made without reference to the people in a general election, but the action of popular sovereignty is much less direct.

This will impose an enforced period of restraint against hurried amendments (although, if an amendment really is urgent, then Parliament may vote, by a two-thirds majority, to dissolve itself; this would expose the Government to the risk of losing its majority, and would, in any case, provide people with an opportunity to reconsider).

## Final Considerations

This final section provides an opportunity to discuss some of the hitherto unexplored themes that, although perhaps somewhat tangential to the actual design of a Model Constitution, are nevertheless vital to the overall project of building a well-constituted Scottish State. These matters need to be raised here only because they are not being raised elsewhere, and it appears that those seeking Scotland's freedom have not fully appreciated the nature, or indeed the difficulty, of the task in which they are engaged.

The first point to consider is that an independent Scotland cannot function well as a one-party State. It is to be expected that independence will be brought about by the SNP, and that the SNP in office will bear a heavy responsibility for guiding the State through its first years. But it would not be healthy for Scotland to know nothing but SNP Governments – even the best parties become corrupt, apathetic, compromised and worn out by too long in power. Sooner or later, a competitive party-system will have to develop, in which the people have an effective choice between sets of alternative policies, programmes and personalities. The shape this will take is beyond speculation – the process of independence, judging by the experience of countries such as Malta and Ireland, tends to re-shape the political landscape, giving birth to new parties or causing old ones to fade away. It is possible to imagine several scenarios. One possibility is that a two-party system develops, with the SNP and Labour competing against each other on grounds of competence and personality, while both having a broadly similar 'centre-left-but-not-socialist' policy stance. These might be flanked by smaller Green, socialist and Conservative parties, which have no chance of forming a Government on their own, but do form free-floating coalitions with one or other of the two main parties. Alternatively, a two-bloc system might emerge, with the SNP moving to the right of centre and Labour to the left, so that competition takes place between a centre-right SNP-Conservative bloc and a centre-left Labour-led bloc. This assumes that the existing parties continue – it is possible that independence, and how to respond to it, could split Labour, and cause a general re-alignment of the left. It is also quite possible that new parties, representing interests or strands of opinion that are at present not salient in Scottish political life, might come to the fore. These might include, for example, a Highlands and Islands Party, a populist party of the free-market right in place of the Conservatives, or a much stronger Green or Eco-communitarian party.

Whatever happens, the crucial point that the Scottish State, if it is to thrive and prosper, cannot belong to one party alone. It has to belong to the whole people, and find room within it for different strands of opinion. The Model Constitution tries to do just that. It offers to minority parties, as well as to those in the majority, a chance to share in power. It gives them a stake in the system, encouraging loyal and responsible opposition rather than obstructionism.

The second point to consider is the international dimension. The political relationship between Scotland and the other countries of these islands is outside the scope of this book, as is the relationship between an independent Scotland and the European Union. Yet, it must be recognised that in today's world no State can be entirely independent. All are locked into a system of interdependent powers and responsibilities. Scotland will, after independence, be free to negotiate and engage with other countries, and, with them, to make treaty arrangements that are of mutual benefit.

This is not restricted to major organisations such as the UN, the EU, NATO and the ('British') Commonwealth – all of which, presumably, an independent Scotland would seek to join or to remain a part of (although, at the time of writing, the future of the EU, in the face of the Greek debt crisis, looks less certain than it has been for decades).

It also extends to other forms of co-operation. It might, for example, be thought expedient to join the Nordic Council. It might even be beneficial to create a new form of union or alliance within the British Isles, perhaps taking the Nordic Council or the Benelux Treaty as its model, to enable certain powers to be shared between Scotland and the rest of (what was) the UK. This latter course might seem like an anathema to some Nationalists – but the key feature of such arrangements is that they would be matters of Scottish foreign policy, and not matters of UK-wide territorial management.

Finally, it must be remembered that the Model Constitution proposed in this book is merely an example of what could be achieved. I believe it to be a good example. However, it does not claim to be perfect, and will not be the final word on the subject. The important point is that we should not confound 'sovereignty of the Scottish Parliament' with 'sovereignty of the Scottish people', nor mistake the achievement of 'mere independence' for greater prize of achieving a firm and lasting democracy.

# End Notes

1  SNP (2002) *A Free Scotland,* Scottish National Party HQ, Edinburgh.
2  MacCormick, N. (2008), personal communication.
3  Crawford, B. (2010), personal communication.
4  The Scottish Government (2009) *Your Scotland, Your Voice.*
5  Agh, A (1998) *The Politics of Central Europe,* Sage Political Texts, pp.87–88.
6  Technically, Dahl uses the term 'Polyarchy' to identify the sort of State found in the Western world today. 'Liberal-Democracy' is just as accurate and more conventional.
7  Lijphart, A. (1999) *Patterns of Democracy,* Yale University Press, pp.48–49.
8  Crick, B. (2002) *Democracy, A Very Short Introduction,* Oxford Paperbacks, pp.107–108.
9  See: Sandel, M. (1998) *Democracy's Discontent: America in Search of a Public Philosophy,* Belknapp, Harvard University Press; Honohan, I. (2002) *Civic Republicanism,* Routledge.
10 Lijphart, A. (1999) *op. cit.* pp.258–274; 293–300.
11 Viroli, M. (2001) *Republicanism,* Hill & Wang.
12 Mill, J. S. (1972), 'Considerations On Representative Government' in Action, H.B. (ed.) *Utilitarianism, On Liberty and Considerations on Representative Government,* Dent: Everyman's Library.
13 Viroli, M. (2001) *op. cit.*
14 A brief list would include Aristotle, Cicero, Polybius, St Thomas Aquinas, Guicciardini, Machiavelli, James Harrington and Thomas Jefferson – as well as modern scholars such as Michael Sandel, Philip Pettit, Richard Dagger, Kevin O'Leary, E F Schumacher and William Everdell.
15 Strøm, K., Müller, W. and Bergman, T. (2005) *Delegation and Accountability in Parliamentary Democracies,* Oxford: Oxford University Press. p.113.
16 Paine, T. (1987) *The Rights of Man.* Penguin. p.220.
17 Paine, T. *ibid.* p.221.
18 Rousseau, J-J. *The Social Contract,* Book III, Chapter 15 available at http://www.constitution.org/jjr/socon_03.htm#015 accessed 11 October 2011.
19 Constant, B. (1988) 'The Spirit of Conquest and Usurpation and their relation to European Civilisation', in Bianca-Maria Fontana (ed.), *Constant: Political Writings,* Cambridge. p.133.
20 Adams, J. C. & Barile, P. (1966) *The Government of Republican Italy,* Houghton Mifflin, Boston; Spotts, F. & Weiser, T. (1986), *Italy: A Difficult Democracy,* Cambridge University Press.

21  Bobbio, N. & Viroli, M. (2003) *The Idea of the Republic*, Polity Press. pp.66–100.

22  Lijphart, A. (1999) *op. cit.* pp.258–274.

23  Lijphart, A. *ibid.* pp.293–300.

24  Lijphart, A. *ibid.* pp.275–292.

25  Lijphart, A. *ibid.*

26  SNP (2002) *op. cit.*4.

27  MacCormick, N. (2008), personal communication.

28  Presidency Conclusions of the Copenhagen European Council, 21–22 June 1993 available at http://www.europarl.europa.eu/enlargement/ec/pdf/cop_en.pdf accessed 11 October 2011.

29  The measurement of democratic quality has produced a broad academic literature. The Economist Intelligence Unit's Democracy Index offers one widely-accepted approach. See also: Beetham, D. (ed.) (1994) *Defining and Measuring Democracy*, Sage Publications.

30  SNP (2002) *op. cit.*

31  MacAskill, K. *Building a Nation: Post Devolution Nationalism in Scotland*, Luath Press, Edinburgh. p. 43.

32  Robert Burns, *A Man's a Man for A'That* available at http://en.wikisource.org/wiki/A_Man%27s_a_Man_for_A%27_That accessed 11 October 2011.

33  Lefebvre, E. (1997) *The Citizen Burgher: The Belgian Constitution of 1831*, discussion paper presented at Zentrum für Europäische Rechtspolitk, Bremen.

34  Interview with Charlie Rose, broadcast on 27 October 1994.

35  SNP (1997) *Citizens not Subjects*, Scottish National Party HQ, Edinburgh.

36  Lijphart, A. (1999) *op. cit.* 150–153.

37  The extent to which this power will, in future, be restrained by the Fixed Term Parliaments Act of 2011 remains to be seen.

38  MacCormick, N. (1991). 'An Idea for a Scottish Constitution'. in Finnie, W., Himsworth, C. M. G. and Walker, N. (eds.), *Edinburgh Essays in Public Law*, Edinburgh University Press. p.159; see also: SNP (1997) *op. cit.*; SNP 2002) *op. cit.*

39  One possibility is that the Consultative Assembly, mentioned under Miscellaneous Provisions below, could, with suitable modifications, be transformed into a fully-fledged second chamber. If expanded to include representatives of local Councils, this would produce a second chamber somewhat akin to the National Council of Slovenia, or to the old Senate of Bavaria (1946–1999). It would also be necessary to give such a second chamber real powers, at least equivalent to those of the minority veto referendum (e.g. power to delay non-financial legislation for at least a year, subject to override by a two-thirds majority vote of the lower House).

40  In practice, these moments of decision will usually be structured through political parties; in most cases, governments take office by winning a parliamentary majority at the ballot box or by building a majority coalition,

and fall only when they lose the trust of their own backbenchers or when a coalition falls apart over some irreconcilable difference. Still, the operative principle is that the government must, ultimately, enjoy the confidence of Parliament if Parliament is to submit to its leadership.

41 Bagehot, W. (1867) *The English Constitution*, available at http://www. gutenberg.org/files/4351/4351-h/4351-h.htm accessed 11 October 2011.

42 Wright, K. (2009), personal communication.

43 Such principled resignations will not be undertaken lightly, of course. The personal sacrifice is great – as Robin Cook, resigning from Tony Blair's government over the decision to invade Iraq, discovered to his cost. Yet the threat of a high-profile resignation remains one of the most effective ways in which a Minister can prevail upon a Prime Minister to reconsider his or her actions.

44 Chubb, B. (1992) *The Government and Politics of Ireland* (Third Edition), Longman. p.188.

45 MacCormick, N. (1991) *op. cit.* p.165.

46 Walker, D. (2007) 'The Union and the Law', Journal Online available at http://www.journalonline.co.uk/Magazine/52-6/1004238.aspx accessed 11 October 2011.

47 Declaration of Arbroath available from the National Archives of Scotland http://www.nas.gov.uk/downloads/declarationArbroath.pdf accessed 11 October 2011.

48 Mill, J. S. (1972) *op. cit.* p. 378.

49 Moos, M. (1945) 'Don Luigi Sturzo: Christian Democrat', *The American Political Science Review*, Vol. 9, No. 2. p.278.

50 Ackerman, B. (2000). 'The new separation of powers', *Harvard Law Review* 113(3), pp.633–729; see also: Pettit, P. (1997). *Republicanism: A Theory of Freedom and Government.* Oxford: Oxford University Press.

51 Ackerman, B. (2000). *op. cit.*

52 In the autumn of 2009, the Guardian newspaper revealed that the Association of Chief Police Officers, a body which has no legal standing, and is not subject to the Freedom of Information Act, has been found to share information on the personal habits of peaceful protestors.

53 See also: Grayling, A. C. (2007) *Towards the Light: The Story of the Struggles for Liberty & Rights That Made The Modern West*, Bloomsbury Publishing, London.

54 Harrington, J. (1656) *The Commonwealth of Oceana* available at http://www.constitution.org/jh/oceana.htm accessed 11 October 2011.

55 Jefferson, T. (1776) *Draft Constitution for Virginia* available at http://avalon.law.yale.edu/18th_century/jeffcons.asp accessed 11 October 2011.

56 Lijphart, A. (1999) *op. cit.* p.2.

# A Model Constitution for Scotland

## Article I – Preliminaries

(1) Scotland is a free, sovereign and independent Commonwealth. Its form of government is a parliamentary democracy based upon the sovereignty of the people, social justice, solidarity and respect for human rights.

(2) This Constitution is the supreme and fundamental law of Scotland: all Acts of Parliament, treaties, regulations, and other laws, that are incompatible with this Constitution, are void.

(3) The territory of Scotland comprises all the mainland and islands of Scotland, plus its territorial waters as recognised by international law.

(4) Citizenship:

   (a) All persons who were British subjects immediately prior to independence, and were born in Scotland, or were resident in Scotland at independence, shall become citizens of Scotland.

   (b) Parliament shall enact laws to regulate the future acquisition of Scottish citizenship by birth, marriage, or naturalisation, and to specify the manner in which citizenship may be lost or renounced.

   (c) Parliament shall specify the circumstances and conditions under which dual citizenship with other countries may be held.

   (d) Laws concerning the acquisition or renunciation of citizenship must not unfairly discriminate on the grounds of gender, ethnicity, religion, beliefs, disability, personal status or sexual orientation.

*Article I – Preliminaries (cont')*

(e) Adopted children shall for purposes of citizenship be treated as though they had been actually
born to their adoptive parents.

(5) Subject only to such further requirements as to
residence as may be prescribed by law, and to such
reasonable restrictions as may be imposed by law
with respect to those persons who are under
guardianship due to severe mental incapacity, or
who are serving a custodial sentence for a serious
criminal offence, all citizens of Scotland, who are at
least 18 years of age, shall be entitled to vote in all
referendums and elections.

# Article II – The Head of State

(1) The office of Head of State shall be vested in Elizabeth
Windsor, and shall be hereditary in her heirs and suc-
cessors, according to the laws of succession, regency
and exclusion enacted by Scotland's Parliament.

(2) The Head of State shall be crowned in Scotland as
'His (or Her) Grace, King (or Queen) of Scots', and
shall be bound by a coronation oath, as prescribed
by Schedule 1(a), to uphold, defend and obey the
Constitution and laws of Scotland.

(3) The Head of State shall be paid a Civil List, as
determined by law, from which the expenses of the
Royal Household in Scotland shall be defrayed. The
royal accounts shall be open to scrutiny by
Parliament.

(4) The Head of State shall possess only such powers
and functions as are expressly vested in him/her by
this Constitution, and shall, where so stated,
exercise these powers and functions solely with the
advice and consent of the responsible constitutional
authorities, as follows:

(a) Representing the liberty, independence and
integrity of the Scottish nation, presiding over
public ceremonies, and addressing the people on
civic occasions and at times of crisis or emergency.

*Article II – The Head of State (cont')*

(b) Dissolving Parliament on the advice of the Presiding Officer in accordance with the provisions of Sections (5) to (8) of Article III.

(c) Granting or withholding assent to legislation, in accordance with the provisions of Section (17) of Article III.

(d) Appointing and dismissing the Prime Minister, in accordance with the provisions of Sections (2) to (6) of Article IV.

(e) Appointing members of the judiciary in accordance with the provisions of Section (3) of Article V.

(f) Granting pardons on the advice of the Minister of Justice in accordance with the provisions of Section (11) of Article V.

(g) Appointing certain members of Independent Commissions in accordance with the provisions of Section (4) of Article VIII.

(h) Acting as Sovereign of the Order of the Thistle, and awarding civic honours, according to law, in recognition of public services.

(i) Serving as the ceremonial Commander-in-Chief of the Armed Forces, accrediting and receiving ambassadors, and performing other associated duties, as directed by the Council of Ministers.

(j) Appointing officers of the Royal Household and Great Officers of State whose appointment is not otherwise provided for by this Constitution or by law.

(k) Attending the General Assembly of the Church of Scotland, in recognition of its legal status as a national church.

(5) During the absence of the Head of State from Scotland, or inability to perform his or her duties, the constitutional powers and functions of the Head of State stated in Section (4) of this Article

*Article II – The Head of State (cont')*

may be delegated by letters patent to a 'Lord High Commissioner', who shall act as the official representative of the Head of State. Subject to any provisions prescribed by law, the Lord High Commissioner shall be appointed by the Head of State, on the joint nomination of the Prime Minister and the Leader of the Opposition, and shall hold office during the Head of State's pleasure. No Member of Parliament, nor Minister, may serve as Lord High Commissioner.

# Article III – Parliament

(1) The supreme legislative power (subject to the provisions of this Constitution) shall be entrusted to a unicameral Scottish Parliament.

(2) Parliament shall be elected by secret ballot using the Mixed Member Proportional system:

    (a) Voters shall have two votes: one for a regional list and one for a constituency candidate.

    (b) Up to 60 per cent of the members shall be elected by plurality voting in single-member constituencies. At least 40 per cent shall be elected from regions of at least six members.

    (c) The total number of seats (including constituency and regional list seats) to be allocated to each party in a region shall be proportional to the share of the list votes received therein, calculated using the D'Hondt formula.

    (d) No artificial threshold for the distribution of regional list seats exceeding four per cent nationally shall be applied.

    (e) Constituency and regional boundaries shall be set by law, on the advice of the Electoral Commission, on the principle of equal population, having due regard for common interests, historical and geographical identities, and existing boundaries.

*Article III – Parliament (cont')*

(3) Every person eligible to vote in elections for the Scottish Parliament, who is at least 21 years of age, subject to such residency rules as may be prescribed by law, shall be eligible for election to Parliament. Provided, however, that no person who holds executive, administrative, military, diplomatic or judicial office (other than Ministerial office) may be elected to Parliament unless they resign from the incompatible office.

(4) The total number of members of Parliament shall be determined by law, but it shall not be fewer than 120 members, nor exceed 200 members.

(5) Parliament shall, except as stated in Sections (6), (7) and (8) of this Article, continue in office for a fixed term of four years; and the Head of State, acting on the advice of the Presiding Officer, shall dissolve each Parliament on the fourth anniversary of the preceding dissolution, and issue writs for a general election to be held within the next thirty days.

(6) If Parliament has failed to elect a Prime Minister within the period of 30 days as specified in Section (3) of Article IV, then the Presiding Officer, after consulting the various parliamentary parties, may advise the Head of State to dissolve Parliament; writs shall thereupon be issued for a general election to be held within a period of 40 days.

(7) If Parliament, by a two-thirds majority vote of its members, passes a resolution calling for its own dissolution, in order to resolve an impasse or to seek a fresh mandate from the people, the Presiding Officer shall advise the Head of State to dissolve Parliament; writs shall thereupon be issued for a general election to be held within a period of 40 days.

(8) Parliament shall have the power, in time of war or public emergency, to extend its term of office for a period not exceeding 12 months, by means of

*Article III – Parliament (cont')*

a resolution passed by a two-thirds majority of its members.

(9) Vacancies in Parliament arising from the death, resignation or removal of a member shall be filled within three months. Unless a general election in due in that time, constituency vacancies shall be filled by a by-election, regional vacancies by re-selection from the appropriate list.

(10) Parliament shall elect from among its members a Presiding Officer and two Deputy Presiding Officers to convene its sessions and enforce its rules of procedure. These officers shall be elected as the first item of business after each general election, and whenever a vacancy occurs, by secret ballot and by an absolute majority. The Presiding Officer, and the Deputy Presiding Officers when in the chair, must perform their duties in a strictly non-partisan manner.

(11) Parliament shall determine its own sessions and adjournments; provided, that it must assemble within seven days after each general election, and it must assemble each year for a regular session of at least 90 days. The Presiding Officer shall summon extraordinary sessions, whenever he/she deems it necessary, or if so demanded by the Council of Ministers, or by one-third of the members of Parliament.

(12) There shall be a Parliamentary Bureau, consisting of the Presiding Officer (as convenor) and one Member of Parliament nominated by each party or group having at least five members of Parliament. The members of the Bureau shall endeavor to reach agreement by consensus, but in the event of a matter being resolved by vote they shall cast bloc votes equal to the number of members they represent, and an absolute majority of the bloc votes cast shall be decisive. The Parliamentary Bureau shall prepare Parliament's agenda and order of business. In the arrangement of parliamentary time, due

*Article III – Parliament (cont')*

precedence shall be given to the legislative proposals and other businesses initiated by the Council of Ministers, but at least one-fourth of the parliamentary time shall be reserved for the opposition and private members' business.

(13) There shall be a Parliamentary Corporate Body, consisting of the Presiding Officer (as convenor), the Deputy Presiding Officers, and four other members of Parliament elected by proportional representation at the commencement of each session. The Corporate Body shall manage Parliament's staff, buildings, facilities, security and budget, and shall propose the rules of procedure, which may be adopted or amended by a two-thirds majority vote of Parliament.

(14) All members of Parliament shall enjoy:

(a) Freedom of speech and debate in Parliament, subject only to Parliament's own rules of procedure (Standing Orders).

(b) Exemption from the law of defamation for anything spoken or written in the course of their duties.

(c) Freedom to vote in accordance with their consciences, free from imperative mandates, binding pledges or intimidation.

(d) Immunity from arrest and imprisonment during sessions of Parliament.

(e) A moderate salary, and other incidental allowances, as prescribed by law.

(15) Subject also to any detailed provisions prescribed by Parliament's rules of procedure, Parliament shall enact laws in the following manner:

(a) Legislative bills may be proposed by the Council of Ministers, by any individual member of Parliament, or by means of a public petition

*Article III – Parliament (cont')*

signed by at least five per cent of the registered voters; provided, that money bills, which shall be limited to matters of taxation and public finance, may only be proposed by a responsible Minister.

(b) The bill shall be debated in Parliament, and if approved by a majority of those voting, it shall be presented to the appropriate select committee of Parliament. The committee shall conduct hearings, to which representations may be made by or on behalf of all persons or groups interested in the subject matter of the bill.

(c) The committee shall report on the bill to Parliament, and shall recommend such amendments as they shall deem necessary or expedient; Parliament shall vote on recommended amendments.

(d) Parliament shall vote upon the bill in the form agreed in the previous stage. The bill shall be deemed to have been passed only if approved by a majority of those present and voting.

(16) Any bill, other than a money bill or bill which is certified as urgent by the unanimous decision of the Parliamentary Bureau, may be suspended by means of a petition to the Presiding Officer:

(a) Such petition shall be signed by two-fifths of the members of Parliament, and presented within ten days of the final vote on the bill. No member of Parliament may, during the same session of Parliament, support more than three suspension petitions.

(b) The period of suspension shall be 12 months from the date of the petition, or until after the next general election, whichever is the sooner.

(c) After the period of suspension has elapsed,

*Article III – Parliament (cont')*

Parliament may reconsider the bill; and if the bill is again passed, by an absolute majority, it shall be presented to the Head of State for assent according to Section (17).

(d) Provided, however, that the Council of Ministers may, at any time before the expiry of the period of suspension, hold a referendum on the bill. If a majority of the votes cast in the referendum are in favour of the bill, the bill shall be submitted for assent under Section (17) without further delay.

(e) If a suspended bill has not been re-passed by Parliament within 18 months of the date of its suspension, or has been submitted to the people and rejected by them, the bill shall lapse, and may not be re-introduced during the same session.

(17) The Head of State, on the advice of the Presiding Officer, shall grant royal assent to, and thus enact as law, all bills passed by Parliament according to the aforesaid provisions; provided, that if the Presiding Officer has any reasonable doubt as to the validity of a bill under the terms of this Constitution, he or she shall not present such bill for royal assent, but shall instead refer it to the Supreme Court for an advisory ruling. The Supreme Court shall examine the bill and issue its advisory ruling within a period of 30 days. If the Supreme Court rules that the bill contains unconstitutional provisions, or has not been passed by the proper constitutional procedure, assent shall be withheld, and the bill shall be returned to Parliament for further consideration; otherwise, the Presiding Officer shall advise the Head of State to grant assent.

(18) No Act of Parliament for the levying of any form of general taxation whatsoever may remain in force for a period longer than 12 months after the date on which

## Article III – Parliament (cont')

such Act came into force. No public funds shall be expended for any purpose, save as authorised by Act of Parliament.

(19) For specified purposes, Parliament may delegate the authority to make regulations, having the force of law, to the Council of Ministers and other public authorities. Regulations shall be laid before Parliament for at least 30 days before they come into effect, and during this time any proposed regulation may be vetoed by a simple majority resolution, on the recommendation of an appropriate select committee. Parliament may not delegate legislative authority concerning the levying of taxation, the creation of new criminal offences, the personal rights of citizens, the principles of civil or criminal law, or the administration of justice; and no regulation shall ever amend, repeal, or suspend, an Act of Parliament.

(20) Parliament shall have the authority to appoint select committees to inspect and oversee the government and to scrutinise legislation. They shall consist of at least 12 members, chosen by a parliamentary vote, by proportional representation.

(21) Parliament may also appoint Royal Commissions and Boards of Enquiry, which may include expert advisors from outside of Parliament, in order to investigate and report on particular decisions or particular aspects of policy, legislation, or administration. Their composition, duration and terms of reference shall be specified by a parliamentary resolution.

(22) Parliamentary committees, Royal Commissions and Board of Enquiry shall enjoy a right of general access to official documents, files and other evidence, and the power to summon Ministers and other officials.

(23) Members of Parliament holding a ministerial office shall, by virtue of that office, be disqualified from membership of all select committees and from

*Article III – Parliament (cont')*

Parliament's Corporate Body. They may serve on Royal Commissions and Boards of Enquiry only where there is no conflict of interest.

(24) Parliament, its committees and commissions, shall be open to the public and press, unless a closed session is authorised, by a two-thirds majority vote, on the grounds of military secrecy or diplomatic security.

(25) The elected leader of the largest parliamentary party or group which is not participating in or supporting the Government, shall be designated by the Presiding Officer as the Leader of the Opposition.

# Article IV – The Council of Ministers

(1) The executive power shall be vested in the Council of Ministers, which shall consist of a Prime Minister, a Deputy Prime Minister, and such other Ministers (including Junior Ministers and Ministers- without-portfolio) as may be required to conduct the Government of the State.

(2) The Prime Minister shall be elected by Parliament from amongst its members, by open ballot and a simple majority vote. The duly elected Prime Minister-designate shall then be appointed by the Head of State.

(3) A Prime Minister shall be elected and appointed within 30 days after each parliamentary general election, and within 30 days after the death, resignation, or removal, of the former Prime Minister; and if a Prime Minister has not been elected during this time, Parliament may be dissolved, in accordance with the provisions of Section (6) of Article III.

(4) The incumbent Prime Minister shall continue in office, following a general election, until their successor be elected and appointed in the manner prescribed in this Article; and during the interval between the death, resignation or removal of a Prime Minister, and the appointment of a successor, the

*Article IV – The Council of Ministers (cont')*

Council of Ministers shall act in a caretaker capacity.

(5) The Prime Minister shall be responsible to Parliament and shall be removed from office by the Head of State if a vote of no-confidence is passed by Parliament by an absolute majority vote.

(6) The Prime Minister may submit his/her resignation to the Head of State on the grounds of illness, incapacity, or other due cause, but the resignation shall become effective only when endorsed by Parliament.

(7) All other Ministers (including the Deputy Prime Minister, Ministers-without-portfolio and Junior Ministers) shall be appointed by the Prime Minister. They serve during the Prime Minister's pleasure, but may be removed by a vote of no-confidence passed by an absolute majority.

(8) The total number of persons holding ministerial office (including the Deputy Prime Minister, Ministers-without-portfolio and Junior Ministers) shall not at any time exceed one-fifth of the membership of Parliament. The Ministers shall be appointed from amongst the members of Parliament; provided, however, that up to one-third of the Ministers may be appointed from outside Parliament, on account of their specialist knowledge, experience, and qualifications. The Ministers appointed from outside Parliament shall have the right, *ex-officio*, to sit and speak (but not vote) in Parliament.

(9) The Council of Ministers, subject to the Constitution and the laws, shall determine all matters of foreign and domestic policy: it shall direct the administration, conduct foreign relations, manage public finances, and ensure that the laws are duly implemented and enforced. It may prepare draft legislation, and other business, to lay before Parliament.

(10) The administrative officials, subordinate to the Council of Ministers, shall be organized as a permanent,

### Article IV – The Council of Ministers (cont')

professional and non-partisan civil service, which shall be based upon merit and shall be regulated by the Public Service Commission in accordance with the law.

(11) High command of the Armed Forces, subject to the Constitution and laws, shall be vested in the Council of Ministers; but no declaration of war may be made, nor deployment of troops undertaken, except with the prior consent of a two-thirds majority of Parliament; provided, that if Scotland is under actual, or imminent, enemy attack, the Council of Ministers shall at once undertake all necessary defensive action.

(12) No treaty or international agreement of any kind shall come into effect unless it is ratified by Parliament (either by a majority resolution or, to the extent that it concerns domestic laws, by enabling legislation). Treaties delegating legislative, administrative, judicial, military or fiscal powers to a confederation, union, alliance or international organisation shall take effect only if ratified by a two-thirds majority of Parliament.

(13) All prerogatives, powers, rights and duties vested in the Crown or in Scottish Ministers according to the law of Scotland immediately prior to the coming into effect of this Constitution shall be transferred to the Council of Ministers herein established, except for such prerogatives, powers, rights and duties as are abolished, or transferred to other bodies, by this Constitution or by any subsequent Act of Parliament.

## Article V – Judiciary

(1) The judicial authority shall be vested in the Supreme Court, the Court of Session, High Court of Justiciary, Sheriff Courts, and such other Courts and Tribunals as may be established by Acts of Parliament.

(2) The Supreme Court shall consist of seven members. It

## Article V – Judiciary (cont')

shall have final appellate jurisdiction over all questions: (i) concerning the validity of Acts of Parliament, treaties, and other laws, under the terms of this Constitution, and (ii) concerning the interpretation of this Constitution. Nothing in Section (17) of Article III shall restrict the ordinary process of constitutional judicial review under this Section.

(3) Judges of the Supreme Court, members of the Court of Session and High Court of Justiciary, Sheriffs, and all other members of the judiciary, with the exception of Justices of the Peace, shall be appointed by the Head of State, on the advice of the Judicial Appointments Council.

(4) The Judicial Appointments Council shall consist of the following members:

(a) The Minister of Justice, as convenor;

(b) The Lord Advocate, as deputy-convenor;

(c) Two Senators of the College of Justice elected by their peers;

(d) A representative of the Faculty of Advocates; and

(e) Five lay representatives of the public, not being members of the judiciary or the legal profession, elected by Parliament, by proportional representation and secret ballot, for four-year terms.

(5) Members of the judiciary shall enjoy security of tenure during good behaviour. They may only be removed on the grounds of misconduct, neglect of duty, or incapacity, by means of a motion of censure passed by a two-thirds majority vote of Parliament, on the advice of the Judicial Appointments Council. The Judicial Appointments Council shall have the authority to suspend a judge, on full pay, for a period of up to three months, pending the outcome of Parliament's decision in his/her case.

*Article V – Judiciary (cont')*

(6) Judicial office shall be incompatible with all other public offices and with membership of any political party. Additional incompatibilities maybe prescribed by Act of Parliament.

(7) The salaries and privileges of members of the judiciary shall be determined by law, and shall not be diminished during their tenure.

(8) Members of the judiciary shall retire, on pensions, on reaching the retirement age prescribed by law. Early retirement may be granted by the Judicial Appointments Council on the grounds of illness or infirmity.

(9) Subject to the provisions of this Constitution, the organisation, powers, structure, jurisdiction, privileges, and procedures of the various Courts shall continue as heretofore, until altered or amended by statute.

(10) The Lord Advocate shall be appointed by the Council of Ministers, after consultation with the Judicial Appointments Council, for renewable four-year terms. The organisation of the Crown Office, and procedures for the appointment of Procurators-Fiscal, shall be determined by law.

(11) The right of pardon, and of remitting punishments, shall be vested in the Head of State, and exercisable upon the advice of the Minister of Justice, given after he or she has considered the recommendations of an independent Pardons Board to be established according to law.

## Article VI – Local Government

(1) For the purposes of local government and administration, Scotland shall be divided by law into Districts and Cities (based, until otherwise provided by law, on the existing unitary boundaries).

(2) Each District and City shall be governed according to

## Article V – Local Government (cont')

law by a Council, consisting a convenient number of councillors, who shall be directly elected by the local enfranchised citizens, by secret ballot and proportional representation, in the manner prescribed by law.

(3) Each District and City Council shall elect from amongst its members a Lord Provost, Provost or Convenor to preside over the Council and to represent the Council in its external affairs. Each Council shall also elect a Leader to act as its executive. Provided, however, that provision may be made by law for the direct election of an 'Executive Provost' to combine these functions.

(4) District and City Councils shall have such legislative, administrative and fiscal powers as may be devolved to them by law, in accordance with the principle of subsidiarity, in relation to: (i) economic development; (ii) housing, land use and planning; (iii) infrastructure; (iv) transport; (v) the upkeep of streets, roads and public spaces; (vi) public health; (vii) the control and recycling of waste; (viii) education and training; (ix) environmental protection; (x) libraries, museums, the arts and culture; (xi) poor relief and social services; (xii) policing and public safety; (xiii) parks, garden and allotments; (xiv) recreational facilities; and (xv) any other matter of local concern.

(5) Districts and Cities may be further sub-divided into Communities and Burghs, each with its own Community or Burgh Council. The boundaries, powers and organisation of the Community and Burgh Councils shall be determined, in accordance with the law, by District and City Councils.

## Article VII – Ombudsman and Auditor-General

(1) There shall be an Ombudsman, whose duty it shall be to examine and investigate all complaints of maladministration, injustice, neglect of duty, incompetence, delay, or mistake, alleged to have been committed by, or to have been caused by the negligence or mistake of, Ministers, civil servants, local Councils, public utilities, or other public authorities.

(2) There shall be an Auditor-General, whose duty it shall be to conduct a thorough audit of the public accounts, to ensure that all public monies are properly accounted for, and are expended only in accordance with the law, and to make recommendations to Parliament for improving the economy of public spending, and for eliminating waste and corruption.

(3) The Ombudsman and Auditor-General shall have such powers, related to the said functions, as may be vested in them by law. In particular, they shall possess full powers of investigation, including access to all records and correspondence, and the right to summon witnesses and hear evidence on oath. They may bring to court any matter requiring legal judgment, and may advise authorities to take disciplinary action or remedial action. They shall submit an annual report of their activities to Parliament, but shall be independent of the Government and all other authorities in the exercise of their functions.

(4) The Ombudsman and Auditor-General shall be nominated by the Presiding Officer on the advice of the Parliamentary Bureau, and shall be appointed by a two-thirds majority vote of Parliament, on a non-partisan basis. They may not simultaneously hold any other public office.

(5) The Ombudsman and Auditor-General shall serve for renewable terms of six years, and may only be removed for misconduct or other cause by a two-thirds majority

*Article VII – Ombudsman and Auditor-General (cont')*

of Parliament. They shall have the same restrictions, privileges, salaries, and pensions, as Supreme Court judges.

# Article VIII – Independent Commissions

(1) There shall be an independent, non-partisan, Open Government Commission, which shall be responsible for ensuring compliance with the freedom of information provisions of Section (17) of Article IX.

(2) There shall be an independent, non-partisan, Electoral Commission, which shall be responsible, in accordance with the law, for: (i) ensuring the free and fair conduct of all elections and referendums; (ii) proposing changes to the boundaries of constituencies and electoral regions; (iii) overseeing registration of voters; (iv) enforcing the laws on campaign spending and on donations to political parties and campaigns; (v) registering political parties and auditing their accounts according to law; and (vi) making recommendations to Parliament concerning the impartial administration of elections and referendums.

(3) There shall be an independent, non-partisan, Public Service Commission, which shall be responsible, in accordance with the law, for: (i) maintaining the impartiality of the civil service; (ii) supervising the recruitment, selection, training, promotion, pay, and discipline of public officials; and (iii) making recommendations to the Council of Ministers for senior civil service appointments and appointments to public bodies.

(4) There shall be an independent, non-partisan Broadcasting Commission, which shall be responsible, in accordance with the law, for the regulation of public broadcasting services.

(5) Each Commission established under this Article shall consist of seven members, of which:

*Article VIII – Independent Commissions (cont')*

(a) Three executive members, including the Convenor, shall be appointed by the Head of State, on the joint nomination of the Prime Minister and the Leader of the Opposition, on merit, according to their qualifications and experience.

(b) Four non-executive members shall be elected by Parliament, by secret ballot and on a non-partisan basis, by single transferable vote, to represent the public interest.

(6) The members of the Commissions established under this Article shall serve for non-renewable terms of six years. They may not simultaneously hold any other public office. They may only be removed for misconduct or other due cause by a two-thirds majority vote of Parliament. Their salaries and allowances shall be fixed by law and in parity to those of members of Parliament.

# Article IX – Fundamental Rights and Freedoms

(1) General provisions:

(a) The following provisions shall have effect for the purpose of guaranteeing the fundamental rights and liberties of all Scottish citizens and all persons within the jurisdiction of Scottish Courts.

(b) The rights and liberties guaranteed shall be enjoyed by all persons without discrimination on grounds such as sex, race, colour, religion, personal beliefs, abilities, status or sexuality.

(c) There shall be no limitation upon their exercise save such as is necessary to prevent or penalise acts by any person or group of persons

*Article IX – Fundamental Rights and Freedoms (cont')*

calculated to infringe or destroy the rights and liberties of other persons or groups, or forcibly to subvert the constitutional order which establishes and guarantees those rights and liberties.

(d) Subject to the qualification mentioned in paragraph (c), no law may be passed which abrogates or derogates from guaranteed rights and liberties, unless passed by way of a constitutional amendment in accordance with Article XI of this Constitution.

(e) Every person shall be granted by a competent court a full and adequate and speedy remedy for any infringement whatsoever of his or her guaranteed rights and liberties.

(f) None of the rights guaranteed in this Article of the Constitution shall be subjected to any restriction or limitation other than as expressly provided, nor shall any such restriction or limitation be applied for any purpose other than that expressly prescribed.

(2) Right to life:

(a) Every person has the right to life. No person shall be condemned to death or executed.

(b) If any person's death occurs as a result of a lawful act of war, or of another person's acting in a manner which is permitted by law and which is no more than necessary to defend a person or persons from unlawful violence, or to effect a lawful arrest or to prevent the escape of a person lawfully detained, the action so taken shall not be rendered unlawful by the fact that death has result from it.

(c) This Section shall not prohibit voluntary euthanasia or the medical termination of pregnancy in accordance with the law.

*Article IX – Fundamental Rights and Freedoms (cont')*

(3) Prohibition of torture:

No person shall be subjected to torture, or to inhuman or degrading treatment or punishment.

(4) Prohibition of slavery and forced labour:

(a) No person shall be held in slavery or servitude, nor shall any person be required to perform forced or compulsory labour.

(b) For the purposes of this provision, 'forced or compulsory labour' shall not include:

(i) Any work, not of a hazardous or degrading nature, required to be done in the ordinary course of detention imposed according to the provisions of Section (5) of this Article, or during conditional release from such detention.

(ii) Any service of a military character or, in case of conscientious objectors, service exacted instead of military service.

(iii) Any service lawfully exacted in case of an emergency or calamity threatening the life or well-being of the community.

(iv) Any work or service which forms part of normal civic obligations.

(5) Personal liberty:

(a) Every person has the right to personal liberty and security, and accordingly no person shall be deprived of liberty save in the following cases and in accordance with the procedures prescribed by the law of Scotland:

(i) In the case of his or her lawful detention in accordance with the sentence passed by a competent Court upon his or her conviction of an offence.

(ii) In the case of his or her lawful arrest or

*Article IX – Fundamental Rights and Freedoms (cont')*

> detention for non-compliance with the
> lawful order of a court.
>
> (iii) In the case of his or her lawful arrest or
> detention upon reasonable suspicion of
> having committed, or being engaged in the
> commission of, or being about to commit, a
> criminal offence under the law of Scotland.
>
> (iv) In the case of detention of a person under
> the age of 16 years by lawful order for the
> purpose of his or her educational supervi-
> sion or personal welfare.
>
> (v) In case of the lawful detention of a person
> who is of unsound mind and danger to
> themselves or others.
>
> (vi) In the case of the lawful arrest of a person
> to prevent his or her unlawfully entering
> Scotland, or of a person against whom
> lawful action is being taken with a view to
> deportation or extradition.

(b) Every person who is arrested or detained shall
be informed, as soon as is possible in the
circumstances of the case, in a language which
he or she understands, of the reason for his or
her arrest or detention and of any charge which
is to be laid against him or her; he or she shall
be entitled to inform a member of his or her
family of his or her whereabouts and of the
stated reason for his or her detention, and shall
be entitled as soon as possible to consult a legal
practitioner.

(c) Every person who is arrested or detained in
accordance with Section (5)(a)(iii) of this Article
shall, wherever it is practicable to do so, be
brought before a competent court not later than
the first lawful day after being taken into
custody, such day not being a public or local
holiday: failing which, he or she shall be

*Article IX – Fundamental Rights and Freedoms (cont')*

brought before a competent court as soon as is possible thereafter.

(d) Every person who is arrested or detained in accordance with Section (5)(a)(iii) of this Article shall be brought to trial as soon as is possible;

no person who has been committed for trial of any offence shall be detained in custody for more than 140 days from the date of such committal, except in so far as the High Court of Justiciary may grant lawful extensions.

(e) Every person who has been deprived of liberty by arrest or detention has the right to petition the Court of Session or High Court of Justiciary for liberation, and shall be liberated by order of the Court as soon as is practicable in the circumstances of the case unless such deprivation of liberty is proven to be lawful; if a person so deprived of liberty is for any reason unable to take proceedings on his or her own behalf any other person who can show good cause for so doing may petition the Court in his or her name to test the lawfulness of any such detention.

(6) Right to fair trial:

(a) Every person has the right to fair and impartial judicial proceedings to determine any question raised by process of law concerning his or her legal rights or obligations, or any criminal charge against him or her.

(b) Every such question or charge shall be heard and determined by the competent court or tribunal established by law. Trials shall be conducted in public and judgment shall be pronounced publicly, except in so far as the law permits a court or tribunal to exclude members

*Article IX – Fundamental Rights and Freedoms (cont')*

of the public from part of such proceedings or to prohibit publication of reports concerning part of such proceedings on all or any of the following grounds:

(i) The protection of national security.

(ii) The prevention of disorder in court.

(iii) The protection of children or young people.

(iv) The protection of the personal privacy of both parties.

(v) In the interests of justice, in circumstances in which publicity would inevitably cause serious prejudice to the fair determination of an issue.

(c) Every person charged with a criminal offence shall be presumed innocent until proved guilty according to law.

(d) Every person charged with a criminal offence has the following rights:

(i) To be informed in detail, as soon as is possible in the circumstances of the case, and in a language which he or she understands, of the charge which is made against him or her.

(ii) To have adequate time and facilities for preparing a defence.

(iii) To defend himself or herself in person or through a legal practitioner of his or her own choosing.

(iv) To such financial assistance as is necessary in the light of his or her means to secure adequate legal assistance if desired.

(v) To examine or have examined witnesses against him or her and to obtain the attendance and examination of witnesses on his or her behalf in the same conditions as witnesses against him or her.

*Article IX – Fundamental Rights and Freedoms (cont')*

      (vi) To have all proceedings in court connected with the charge against him or her translated by a competent interpreter into the language which he or she best understands, if that language is not the language of the Court.

     (vii) To be informed in a language which he or she understands of his or her rights under this Sections (5) and (6) of this Article, before the commencement of the trial.

(e) Everyone convicted of a criminal offence by a tribunal shall have the right to have his conviction or sentence reviewed by a higher tribunal. The exercise of this right, including the grounds on which it may be exercised, shall be governed by law. This right may be subject to exceptions in regard to offences of a minor character, as prescribed by law, or in cases in which the person concerned was tried in the first instance by the highest tribunal or was convicted following an appeal against acquittal.

(f) No one shall be liable to be tried or punished again in criminal proceedings for an offence for which he has already been finally acquitted or convicted in accordance with the laws of Scotland. Provided, that this provision shall not prevent the reopening of the case in accordance with the law and penal procedure of Scotland, if there is evidence of new or newly discovered facts, or if there has been a fundamental defect in the previous proceedings, which could affect the outcome of the case.

(g) The right to trial by jury, as such right existed under the law of Scotland at the time of the ratification of this Constitution shall not be suspended, restricted or abridged.

*Article IX – Fundamental Rights and Freedoms (cont')*

(7) No punishment without law:

No person shall be convicted of any criminal offence save in respect of an act or omission which, at the date of its commission, constituted a criminal offence under the law of Scotland or the law of nations, nor shall any penalty be imposed which is heavier than the maximum permitted under the law of Scotland at that date.

(8) Right to respect for private and family life:

(a) Everyone has the right to respect for privacy in his or her personal affairs, family life, home, and correspondence.

(b) There shall be no interference with the exercise of this right except such as is in accordance with the law and is necessary in a democratic society in the interests of national security or public safety, for the prevention of disorder or crime, for the protection of health or morals, or for the protection of the rights and freedoms of others.

(c) Every person who suffers unlawful interference with his or her personal privacy shall be entitled to an adequate civil remedy therefore.

(d) Provision shall be made by law for the safeguarding of personal data and information, and in particular to preserve the privacy and security of all communications and transactions conducted by electronic media.

(9) Freedom of thought, conscience and religion:

(a) Every person has the right to freedom of thought and of conscience and to the free confession and practice of religion. This right includes freedom to change his or her religion or belief and freedom (either alone or in

*Article IX – Fundamental Rights and Freedoms (cont')*

community with others and in public or private)
to manifest his or her religion or belief in worship,
teaching, practice and observance. It also includes
freedom not to believe or participate in any
religion.

(b) Freedom to manifest one's religion or beliefs shall
be subject only to such limitations as are
prescribed by law and necessary in a democratic
society in the interests of public safety, or for the
protection of public order, health or morals.

(c) Nothing in this Section shall affect the existing
status, freedom or liberties of the Church of
Scotland, as recognized by the Church of Scotland
Act 1921 and by the Articles Declaratory of the
Constitution of the Church of Scotland in Matters
Spiritual.

(10) Freedom of expression:

(a) Every person has the right to freedom of speech,
writing and publication, and of the expression of
opinion, including the right to impart and
receive information and ideas freely to and from
any other person or persons whatsoever.

(b) Provided, however, that the law may prohibit
abuses of this right, to the extent necessary in a
democratic society, in the interests of national
security or public safety, for the prevention of
disorder or crime, for the protection of health or
morals, for the protection of the reputation or
rights of others, for preventing the unlawful
disclosure of personal or private information
received in confidence, or for maintaining the
authority and impartiality of the judiciary.

(c) The foregoing provisions shall not be interpreted
as invalidating laws regulating the  licensing of
broadcast transmissions or cinemas, theatres and
other like places of public resort.

*Article IX – Fundamental Rights and Freedoms (cont')*

(11) Freedom of assembly and association:

(a) Every person has the right to freedom of peaceful assembly and to freedom of association with others for all lawful purposes; this right shall include, but not be limited to, the freedom to freely form and to join political parties and trade unions.

(b) The right to freedom of assembly and of association shall be subject only to such restrictions as are prescribed by law and are necessary in a democratic society for the protection of national security, the prevention of crime or disorder, or the protection of the rights of others.

(12) Freedom of movement:

(a) Everyone lawfully within the territory of a Scotland shall, within that territory, have the right to liberty of movement and freedom to choose his residence, and shall have the freedom to leave the country at will.

(b) No restrictions shall be placed on the exercise of these rights other than such as are in accordance with law and are necessary in a democratic society in the interests of national security or public safety, for the prevention of crime or disorder, for the protection of public health, or for the protection of the rights and freedoms of others.

(c) Everyone in Scotland has the right of free access to hills, mountains, waterways and open countryside, except in cases in which unrestricted access is likely to cause substantial interference with agriculture, forestry or fishing, and subject to any provisions of the law which are necessary for the protection of national security or public safety, for the protection of

*Article IX – Fundamental Rights and Freedoms (cont')*

public health, or for the protection of the physical environment.

(13) No imprisonment for debt:

No one shall be deprived of his liberty merely on the ground of inability to fulfil a contractual obligation.

(14) No compulsory expulsion:

(a) No Scottish citizen shall be expelled, by means either of an individual or of a collective measure, from the territory of Scotland.

(b) No Scottish citizen shall be deprived of the right to enter Scotland.

(c) The collective expulsion of aliens is prohibited.

(15) Familial rights:

Men and women of marriageable age have the right to marry and to found a family in accordance with the laws governing the exercise of this right.

(16) Property rights:

(a) Every person has the right to hold private property, and to the peaceful enjoyment of his or her property.

(b) Parliament may, however, enact laws that control or restrict the use or acquisition of property in the general interest, in cases where Parliament determines that the needs of the community require to be given precedence over the rights of individuals.

(c) All laws which sanction measures of expropriation shall make provision for fair compensation.

(d) Nothing in this Article shall have the effect of invalidating any tax, duty or custom levied in

*Article IX – Fundamental Rights and Freedoms (cont')*

accordance with the law, or the lawful collection of any service charge or administrative
fee, or the lawful imposition of a criminal
penalty of fine or forfeiture.

(17) Freedom of Information:

Every person shall have the right of access to
governmental information. The right of access to
official information can only be restricted by law to
the extent necessary, in a democratic society, for the
purpose of protecting personal privacy, national
security or diplomatic confidentiality, or for
ensuring the due process of judicial proceedings.

(18) Economic and Social Rights:

(a) Every person has the right to work and to
pursue freely any profession or vocation
subject only to such requirements as to
minimum qualifications as may be prescribed
by or in accordance with the law.

(b) Every person has the right to conditions of
work which are fair, healthy, and which respect
the dignity of the person. In particular,
Parliament shall ensure by means of
appropriate legislation that every worker has
the following rights, which may not be
renounced by any contractual provision:

(i) Safe and healthy conditions of work.

(ii) An adequate minimum wage as
determined by law.

(iii) Protection against arbitrary or unfair
dismissal.

(iv) Maximum working hours, and minimum
entitlements to days of rest and holidays,
sufficient to maintain health and to meet
obligations of family life.

*Article IX – Fundamental Rights and Freedoms (cont')*

> (v) The right to bargain collectively and to enforce collective bargains through strike action, except in the armed forces, police and essential public services.
>
> (vi) Freedom from harassment, intimidation, humiliation or abuse in the workplace.

(c) Every person who is unable to work by reason of physical or mental disability or infirmity, or by reason of family commitments, or because suitable employment is presently unavailable in their community, has a right to be provided with benefit payments or other social assistance as determined in accordance with the law.

(d) Parliament shall be responsible for ensuring by legislation that all persons who have reached the age of retirement fixed by law are entitled to pensions adequate for their dignity and well-being.

(e) Parliament shall be responsible for ensuring by legislation that everyone has a right to adequate health care sufficient to secure well-being and human dignity; Parliament shall ensure that health services are properly regulated and maintained, and that a system of universal health care, to the highest practicable standards of medical practice, is available to all.

(f) Parliament shall responsible for ensuring by legislation that everyone has a right to a good education; Parliament shall ensure that adequate provision is made for universal primary and secondary education, and that qualified students are entitled to publicly funded tuition and other means of financial support at institutions of higher learning, technical training and research.

(g) Parliament may regulate commerce for the common good, and in particular shall have the authority to enact laws protecting workers, consumers and the environment.

## Article X – Miscellaneous Provisions

(1) All Ministers, members of Parliament, judges, and all other persons holding public office under this Constitution, shall take an oath or affirmation in the form prescribed by Schedule 1(b).

(2) The City of Edinburgh shall be the capital of Scotland; the seat of government may be moved to another place by a decision of the Council of Minister in the event of war, disaster or unrest.

(3) The official languages of Scotland shall be English, Scots and Gaelic. Parliament shall be responsible for ensuring that provision is made for the use of Scots and Gaelic, in addition to English, in parliamentary proceedings, local government, administration, public broadcasting and education.

(4) The national flag is the cross of St Andrew, blazoned *azure, a saltire argent*. The national anthem shall be determined by Act of Parliament.

(5) Persons holding public office should perform their duties solely for the public interest. They should not seek financial or other material benefits for themselves, their family, or friends, nor place themselves under any financial or other obligation to individuals or organisations that might unduly influence them in the performance of their official duties. They have a duty to declare any private interests relating to their public duties and to take steps to resolve any conflicts arising in a way that protects the public interest. To give effect to these and other relevant principles of good conduct, the Public Service Commission shall adopt a Code of Conduct for public servants, including Ministers and those holding elective office. Parliament shall have the authority to enforce observance of the Code of Conduct by means of legislation.

(6) In addition to binding legislative referendums held under Section (16)(d) of Article III and constitutional referendums held under Section (2) of Article XI,

## Article X – Miscellaneous Provisions (cont')

provision may be made by law for the holding of consultative referendums, at the initiative of Parliament or local Councils, on proposed legislation or matters of general policy within their respective areas of competency.

(7) There shall be a Consultative Assembly to advise and assist Parliament and the Council of Ministers on matters of legislation and policy. It shall examine and give its advice on all bills and policy papers submitted to it by Parliament or the Council of Ministers. It may also submit petitions and recommendations to Parliament and the Council of Ministers on its own initiative. The Consultative Assembly shall consist of sixty members appointed in the manner prescribed by law on a vocational and functional basis: (i) 20 shall represent trade unions and craft and artisan guilds; (ii) ten shall represent chambers of commerce and small businesses; (iii) ten shall represent academia and the learned professions; (iv) ten shall represent farmers, crofters and rural interests, and (v) ten shall represent religious and charitable organisations.

(8) The Prime Minister may appoint a number of Special Advisors, not exceeding 12, to advise and assist the Prime Minister in the preparation and delivery of policies. Special Advisors shall serve at the pleasure of the Prime Minister. They shall not be members of the permanent civil service, nor members of Parliament, but are subject to the Code of Conduct for public servants.

(9) The rights and privileges guaranteed to persons under this Constitution or any law extend only to human beings; the extent to which such rights and privileges may be extended to corporate bodies and other 'legal persons', on the grounds of public benefit, shall be determined by law.

(10) In times of war or other severe public emergency the

*Article X – Miscellaneous Provisions (cont')*

Council of Ministers may declare a State of
Emergency. The State of Emergency shall lapse
after seven days, unless during that time
Parliament passes a resolution, by a two-thirds
majority, authorising its extension for up to three
months; such authorisation may be renewed at
intervals of three months, so long as the emergency
necessitating it continues. During a State of
Emergency the Council of Ministers shall have the
authority to enact decrees, having the force of law;
such decrees may suspend rights guaranteed by
Sections (5)(c) and (6)(g) of Article IX and may
impose further restrictions on guaranteed rights
according to Sections (8)(b), (10)(b), (11)(b) and
(12)(b) of Article IX. All decrees shall be subject to
review and veto, on the grounds that they are
unconstitutional, or unnecessarily burdensome or
oppressive, by a Review Committee consisting of
the Presiding Officer, two Supreme Court judges,
and 12 members of Parliament, not holding
ministerial office, elected by their peers by proportional representation.

# Article XI – Adoption and Amendment of the Constitution

(1) Every law in force in Scotland when this
Constitution comes into effect, with the exception
of provisions inconsistent with this Constitution,
shall remain in force until repealed or amended by
a competent legislative act. The first parliamentary
elections shall take place within three months of the
coming into effect of this Constitution; until such
elections, the existing Scottish Parliament shall
remain in being as the interim Parliament of
Scotland under this Constitution.

(2) This Constitution may be amended only if a
proposal for its amendment is adopted by a

*Article XI – Adoption and Amendment of the Constitution (cont')*

two-thirds majority of the whole membership of Parliament and if the amendment is then ratified by the people in a binding nationwide referendum. The referendum shall take place on the date of the next general election. No amendment shall come into effect unless approved by a majority of all valid votes cast in the referendum. No amendment may be proposed, adopted or ratified during the occupation of the country by enemy forces, nor during a State of Emergency.

## Schedule 1

Oaths (or affirmations)

a  *Coronation oath of the King (or Queen) of Scots*

I............................... solemnly swear (or affirm) that I will faithfully execute the office and perform the functions of King (or Queen) of Scots, and that I will, to the best of my ability uphold, defend and obey the Constitution and laws of Scotland. (So help me God).

b  *Oath of office*

I .............................. solemnly swear (or affirm) that I will bear true faith and allegiance to the people of Scotland, and that I will faithfully and conscientiously perform my duties as [name or title of the office to which appointed or elected] in accordance with the Constitution and the laws of Scotland, without fear or favour. (So help me God).

These oaths may be taken with or without religious invocation.

# Some other books published by **LUATH** PRESS

**Scotland: A Suitable Case for Treatment**
Tom Brown and Henry McLeish
ISBN 978-1906307-69-1 PBK £9.99

**Scotlands of the Mind**
Angus Calder
ISBN 978-1842820-08-7 PBK £9.99

**Radical Scotland: Arguments for Self-Determination**
Edited by Gerry Hassan and Rosie Ilett
ISBN 978-1906817-94-7 PBK £12.99

**A Nation Again: Why Independence will be good for Scotland (and England too)**
Edited by Paul Henderson Scott
ISBN 978-1906817-67-1 PBK £7.99

**The Scottish Parliament 1999–2009: The First Decade**
Edited by Charlie Jeffery, James Mitchell
ISBN 978-1906817213 PBK £9.99

**Trident and International Law: Scotland's Obligations**
Rebecca Johnson and Angie Zelter
ISBN 978-1906817-24-4 PBK £12.99

**Agenda for a New Scotland: Visions of Scotland 2020**
Kenny MacAskill
ISBN 978-1905222-00-1 PBK £9.99

**Building a Nation: Post Devolution Nationalism in Scotland**
Kenny MacAskill
ISBN 978-1842820-81-0 PBK £4.99

**Global Scots: Voices from Afar**
Kenny MacAskill and Henry McLeish
ISBN 978-1905222-37-7 PBK

**Wherever the Saltire Flies**
Kenny MacAskill and Henry McLeish
ISBN 978-1905222-68-1 PBK £8.99

**The Warriors and Wordsmiths of Democracy: The Birth and Growth of Democracy**
Linda MacDonald-Lewis
ISBN 978-1906307-27-1 PBK £6.99

**Getting it Together: The History of the Campaign for a Scottish Assembly/Parliament 1980–1999**
Bob McLean
ISBN 978-1905222-02-5 PBK £12.99

**Scotland: The Road Divides**
Henry McLeish and Tom Brown
ISBN 978-1906307-24-0 PBK £8.99

**Voyage of Intent: Sonnets and Essays from the Scottish Parliament**
James Robertson
ISBN 978-1905222-26-1 PBK £6.99

**Scotlands of the Future: Sustainability in a small nation**
Edited by Eurig Scandrett
ISBN 978-1842820-35-3 PBK £7.99

**Great Scottish Speeches**
David Torrance
978-1906817-97-8 HBK £16.99

**The Price of Scotland: Darien, Union and the Wealth of Nations**
Douglas Watt
ISBN 978-1906307-09-7 PBK £9.99

**Scotland: Land and Power – agenda for land reform**
Andy Wightman
ISBN 978-0946487-70-7 PBK £5.00

**Reportage Scotland: Scottish History in the Voices of Those Who Were There**
Louise Yeoman
ISBN 978-1842820-51-3 PBK £7.99

Details of these and other books published by Luath Press can be found at:
**www.luath.co.uk**

## **Luath** Press Limited
*committed to publishing well written books worth reading*

LUATH PRESS takes its name from Robert Burns, whose little collie Luath (*Gael.*, swift or nimble) tripped up Jean Armour at a wedding and gave him the chance to speak to the woman who was to be his wife and the abiding love of his life. Burns called one of 'The Twa Dogs' Luath after Cuchullin's hunting dog in Ossian's *Fingal*. Luath Press was established in 1981 in the heart of Burns country, and now resides a few steps up the road from Burns' first lodgings on Edinburgh's Royal Mile.
Luath offers you distinctive writing with a hint of unexpected pleasures.

Most bookshops in the UK, the US, Canada, Australia, New Zealand and parts of Europe either carry our books in stock or can order them for you. To order direct from us, please send a £sterling cheque, postal order, international money order or your credit card details (number, address of cardholder and expiry date) to us at the address below. Please add post and packing as follows: UK – £1.00 per delivery address; overseas surface mail – £2.50 per delivery address; overseas airmail – £3.50 for the first book to each delivery address, plus £1.00 for each additional book by airmail to the same address. If your order is a gift, we will happily enclose your card or message at no extra charge.

**Luath** Press Limited
543/2 Castlehill
The Royal Mile
Edinburgh EH1 2ND
Scotland
Telephone: 0131 225 4326 (24 hours)
Fax: 0131 225 4324
email: sales@luath.co.uk
Website: www.luath.co.uk